MW01047425

Easter Programs for the Church

compiled by

Pat Fittro

STANDARD
PUBLISHING
Cincinnati, Ohio

Permission is granted to reproduce these programs
for ministry purposes only—not for resale.

Scripture quotations marked (NIV) are taken from the HOLY BIBLE,
NEW INTERNATIONAL VERSION®. NIV®. Copyright © 1973,
1978, 1984 by International Bible Society. Used by permission of
Zondervan Publishing House. All rights reserved.

The Standard Publishing Company, Cincinnati, Ohio
A division of Standex International Corporation
© 1998 by The Standard Publishing Company
All rights reserved. Printed in the United States of America

ISBN 0-07847-0912-2

Contents

In Loving Memory

Debra F. Kelley

Easter Mourning. The occupants of a locked room are exposed to the view of the audience, as each relates a personal memory of Jesus. The experiences and emotions are revealed one by one and shared by all.

This memorial contains drama, occasional humor, and a surprise ending. It is simple to stage and allows for minimal group practice. The effective presentation of this play does not require memorization of the parts or any previous drama experience for most of the participants. Narratives may be rearranged or deleted and music may be added to suit the desires of the group. These features make this play versatile enough to meet the needs of any size congregation.

Characters: *(Listed in suggested order.)*
Narrator—Introduction
James
John
The Delivered Son
Simon Peter's Mother-in-law
Simon Peter
Adulterous Woman
Nathanael
Child
Martha
Mary, Lazarus's Sister
Lazarus
Paralytic Man
Mary, Jesus' Mother
Luke
Boy
Woman healed of the issue of blood
Zacchaeus
Matthew
Jairus's Daughter
Philip
Thomas
Nicodemus

Mary Magdalene
Narrator or Pastor—Optional ending
Musicians and/or nonspeaking cast members may be added but
total cast should not exceed 120 (excluding Narrator).

Setting: Cast is seated on individual chairs or bench seats placed at a
right angle to audience. If space permits, arrange seating with an
aisle down the center. A lectern or table may be placed in front of
cast to represent the front of the room. Individual cast members face
the remainder of the cast (not the audience) while speaking.

Costumes: Mourning attire or dress appropriate for biblical characters; if desired, apron for Martha.

Music: *(Optional)* Many songs are appropriate and may be sung between speaking parts. Care should be taken to choose music that
does not mention the resurrection, or to exclude those specific verses
until after Mary Magdalene's part. Music suggestions are listed at
the end of the program.

Special Instructions: The speaking order may be rearranged as desired *(with the exclusion of the Narrator, James, and Mary Magdalene)*. It
may be helpful to seat characters in speaking and/or singing order.

NARRATOR *(standing in front of or overlooking the set and facing the audience):* Ladies and gentlemen, welcome to *(name of your church)*. We
are pleased that you came today to share in this special service
commemorating our Lord and Savior, Jesus Christ.

We are privileged today to look in on the friends and family of
Jesus as they pay tribute to Him after His death on the cross and
burial in the tomb. Remember that they didn't understand what
had actually taken place, even though Jesus tried to prepare them.
They were not able to see beyond the present circumstances. They
were confused. They were hurting, and they were scared.

Now we present *In Loving Memory*—a memorial service taking
place in a locked room. *(Takes a seat with the audience.)*

JAMES *(Walking to front of room, looking carefully over the group, nodding
to acknowledge some of those present. Looks down, takes a deep breath,
begins a little reluctantly.):* We have gathered here today in respect
of our dear departed loved one—Jesus Christ the Lord. It is fitting

that we, who were his family and disciples and friends, assemble together to pay this final tribute to His memory and to share our grief.

Let us draw comfort from God's Word.

"Lord, thou hast been our dwelling place in all generations. Before the mountains were brought forth, or ever thou hadst formed the earth and the world, even from everlasting to everlasting, thou art God" (Psalm 90:1, 2).

"God is our refuge and strength, a very present help in trouble" (Psalm 46:1).

Let us pray. *(Bowing head.)* Heavenly Father, our hearts are heavy today as we mourn the loss of Your Son. We don't understand what has happened, but we know He promised to do Your will and that Your ways are far beyond our ways. So we now commit all things into Your care. *(Pauses.)* "Our Father which art in heaven, Hallowed be thy name. *(First row join in unison.)* Thy kingdom come. *(James continues. First and second rows in unison.)* Thy will be done in earth, as it is in heaven. *(First, second, and third rows in unison.)* Give us this day our daily bread. *(All in unison to end of prayer.)* And forgive us our debts, as we forgive our debtors. And lead us not into temptation, but deliver us from evil: For thine is the kingdom, and the power, and the glory, for ever. Amen" (Matthew 6:9-13).

(Pause, as if attempting to compose self.) Jesus was born in Bethlehem. His mother Mary, a virgin, found favor with God and conceived by the Holy Ghost while she was espoused to Joseph. In obedience to a decree by Caesar Augustus and because Joseph was of the lineage of David, they had gone to Bethlehem to be taxed. While they were there, Jesus was born. He grew up in Nazareth and worked in the family carpenter shop until He was thirty. The past three years He had traveled with His disciples throughout Palestine and Jerusalem. He spoke of and demonstrated the mercy, love, and power of God the Father to everyone. He influenced and changed lives wherever He went. This Jesus of Nazareth was like no one we have ever seen or even heard about. Would any of you like to share your memories of Jesus? *(Returns to seat.)*

JOHN *(walking to front):* The day I met Jesus, my *(Pointing to James.)* brother James and I were sitting in the ship with our father, Zebedee, mending the nets. He called to us, "Come and follow me and I will make you fishers of men." We dropped the nets and eagerly accepted His invitation.

We watched and learned as He ministered to everyone, even the

Samaritans. Anyone who would listen! Time after time He spoke with such wisdom and authority that the Pharisees and the Sadducees were amazed. But they became increasingly jealous and sought to destroy Him.

I was so happy the day He rode into Jerusalem on a colt and the people were all crying, "Hosanna: blessed is the King of Israel that cometh in the name of the Lord!" I thought it was the beginning of the kingdom Jesus had spoken of so often. *(Shaking head sadly.)* How wrong I was! Just a few days later, some of the very same people who had been waving palm branches and shouting, "Hosanna in the Highest", were waving their fists and screaming, "Crucify Him!" *(Louder, emphatically.)* "Crucify Him!" *(Pauses.)* I watched helplessly as He was betrayed, beaten, spit on, crowned with thorns, mocked, and nailed to a cross between two common thieves. *(Continues.)* Stunned, I heard Him cry out, "It is finished." And—He—died. *(Lovingly.)* I miss Him so much! *(Returns to seat.)*

THE DELIVERED SON *(walks to front and begins speaking peacefully):* Relief! Finally, sweet, wonderful rest!

Only someone who has experienced the deliverance power of Jesus could begin to understand why I just lay there. I was so quiet and still, I could hear the people murmuring, "He's dead."

(Anxious to explain.) Life had not been very good for me. As far back as I could remember, I couldn't hear, I couldn't speak. I had been burned, almost drowned, bruised, and cut repeatedly as a result of frequent convulsions.

Out of desperation, my father took me to Jesus and begged Him to cast out the spirit that tormented me. Jesus said, "If you can believe, all things are possible to him that believeth." My father answered, "I have faith. Help me to have more." Then Jesus rebuked that spirit. It shook me violently one last time and threw me on the ground. Then it was gone! What wonderful peace!

I just lay there quietly, listening and thinking that if I was dead, as those people were saying, then it was better than the life I had known. But Jesus reached down, tugged on my hand, and I stood up. *(Continues, jubilantly.)* I was alive! I could hear! I could talk! I was free! Free! Jesus the Great Deliverer, that's who He will always be to me! *(Returns to seat.)*

SIMON PETER'S MOTHER-IN-LAW *(walking to front, speaking serenely):* I was dreaming. Not of pleasant things. They were strange dreams. Nightmares. Hallucinations. The kind of things you see when you have a very high fever. I was so physically weak and mentally troubled that at first I thought Jesus was just a part of the pictures that kept racing through my mind. Then He laid His cool fingers gently across my fevered brow. Instantly, the fog that had enveloped me dissipated. And the fever that had been raging out of control only moments before was completely gone. *(Smiles.)* I felt rejuvenated, bursting with energy. *(Chuckles.)* So I got up and prepared a meal for Peter and his guests. Jesus wasn't a figment of my imagination. Real. That's what He was to me. Jesus was Real!! *(Returns to seat.)*

SIMON PETER *(walking to front):* Simon Peter "The Rock"—that's what He called me. *(Pauses and shakes head.)* He seemed so sincere, but surely He was joking. I'm a failure. How could I have been so weak after all He did for me? He was always there when I needed Him most, like the time He healed my mother-in-law. And I recollect how patiently He taught and set the example: forgiving, serving, healing, and loving.

We shared so many special moments, such as the time He allowed me to walk on the water. He knew me better than I know myself. I have good intentions but I always seem to be doing and saying the wrong things. I even fell asleep in the Garden of Gethsemane after He had asked me to watch and pray. *(With growing self-reproach.)* Oh, and then when the officers from the chief priests and Pharisees came to take Jesus away, I cut off one man's ear. *(Defensively.)* I was just trying to protect Him. *(With an attitude of defeat.)* But I must have been wrong again, because Jesus healed him.

I thought I could be strong like "The Rock" He wanted me to be. But I denied Him—not just once, not even twice, but **three** times. *(Pauses, then continues sorrowfully.)* And now He's gone! *(With deep remorse.)* I can't even tell Him how very sorry I am. *(Pauses.)* I wish I could have just one more chance to prove how much I love Him! *(Returns to seat.)*

ADULTEROUS WOMAN *(walking to front, with an attitude of true humility):* I had no idea that I would live to talk about the day I met Jesus.

I had been caught in the sin of adultery. I was terrified because I knew that according to the law of Moses, I would be stoned to death.

My accusers brought me before Jesus and demanded to hear His opinion of my punishment. Then He did the strangest thing. Why,

He just ignored them, stooped down, and wrote upon the ground. But they just kept on asking Him again and again, "What sayest thou?" *(Louder.)* "What sayest thou?"

Finally, He stood up and answered, "He that is without sin among you, let him cast the first stone." Then He stooped down and started writing on the ground again.

I could hardly believe my eyes! They left! Incredibly, one by one, **all** of my accusers walked away!

There I stood trembling and alone before Jesus, not knowing what to expect. *(Continues.)* Astonished, I saw His eyes. They weren't filled with contempt, as I had expected. As I stood and gazed into eyes that seemed to overflow with pure, unfathomable love; I heard Jesus say, "Neither do I condemn thee: go, and sin no more."

I was guilty. But Jesus saved my life and set me free. *(Returns to seat.)*

NATHANAEL *(walking to front):* Philip came to me all excited and told me that they had found the One that Moses and the prophets had written about. Said His name was Jesus of Nazareth, the son of Joseph. I had my doubts about that, so I asked, "Can any good thing come out of Nazareth?" Philip smiled and challenged me to come and see. Later, as we walked toward Jesus, He called me by name and let me know I had been revealed to Him in a vision while Philip and I stood talking under the fig tree. Then I replied, "I believe You are the Son of God." *(Reflectively.)* He promised that we would see great things. *(Positively.)* And we have.

(Puzzled.) But He also said that we would see the heavens open and the angels of God ascending and descending upon Him. I thought that they were coming. I expected them to come any moment to stop the mockery and the beatings during His trials. But they didn't come. I looked for them when He fell beneath the weight of the cross as He struggled up Calvary's hill. But the angels weren't there either. *(Emphatically.)* I anxiously waited for the moment they would arrive to take the nails from His hands and feet, remove Him from that cross, and shout to the world, "This is the Son of God!" *(With anguish.)* Where were the angels? Why didn't they come? *(Returns to seat.)*

CHILD *(walking to front):* I know I'm just a small child. But Jesus made me feel very special.

He was the best storyteller. And His stories weren't about dumb things like monsters and witches. Nah, they were about the animals and the flowers and rocks and people. Things you see every day.

My mom says that His stories are pare—paral—I think she said pearbulls. . . . Anyway, you can learn things from them.

One day He held me in His arms and told the disciples that anyone who received a child in His name, received Him and the One who sent Him. He who is least among you—shall be great.

I'm not sure what that means, but I'll remember it. I'll remember all of His stories too. And when I grow up, maybe I can understand.

I don't know why they killed Him. He didn't do anything wrong! Why did He have to die? *(Returns to seat.)*

MARTHA *(Still wearing an apron, rushes into the scene at the very last minute, after everyone else is in place. Rearranges chair slightly, then sits down. When it is time to speak, stands up and straightens clothing. Notices apron and removes it. Walks to front. Begins distractedly.):* I'm sorry I was a little late this morning. The time just slipped up on me. Seems like I always see one or two more little things that need doing.

Jesus warned me. He tried to tell me that I needed to stop and listen. I know He understood that I was expressing my love for Him by cleaning and cooking. If I had only known how soon He would be taken from us, I could have tried harder, let some things go so I could have spent more time with Him.

Jesus was wonderful. I feel so humble and privileged to have known Him and to have served Him. And I really am going to take His advice and slow down a little, like Mary. *(Nodding.)* To-morrow. *(Shaking head.)* No, I must start that spring-cleaning. *(Shrugs shoulders.)* Well, maybe next week. *(Faltering.)* Or the week after that. Or . . . oh, . . . uh . . . *(Mumbling and embarrassed, with head bowed returns to seat.)*

MARY, LAZARUS'S SISTER *(walking to front, melancholic):* Many times Jesus visited in our home. He loved us, and Lazarus, Martha, and I loved Him too. *(Smiling.)* I recall His tenderness. He had such compassion! I will always treasure the memory of how He wept with me as I mourned over Lazarus' death—even though He must have known He was going to call my brother back from the grave.

He shared such wisdom and truth. Spoke with authority. And yet, with such love that every word painted a picture in your mind. *(Pause, as if searching for the correct words.)* Like a living thing. *(Excitedly.)* That's it! Like the Living Word of God! I could just sit and listen to Him for hours.

He defended me when Martha complained that I wasn't helping her serve. And again when I felt moved to anoint His feet and wipe them with my hair. He told Judas to let me alone, that against the day of His burying I had kept that offering. *(Pauses.)* I didn't realize what He meant or that it would be so soon. *(Slowly, sadly.)* And now, He is buried. *(Returns to seat.)*

LAZARUS *(walking to front, admiringly):* He was the best friend I ever had, the wisest person I've ever known, and He was truly the Son of God. No one else could have wakened me from the dead. He called, "Lazarus, come forth"—and I live again! *(Pauses, then continues in a puzzled tone.)* How could He have the power to raise me from the dead—and yet not be able to save himself? *(Returns to seat.)*

PARALYTIC MAN *(While walking to front, greets a couple of the men. Shakes hands with one, pats another on the back. Speaks with earnest gratitude.):* Praise God for friends who really care. If it had not been for the faith and determination of the four men who took me to Him, I doubt whether I would have had the opportunity to even see Jesus from afar.

I was paralyzed and those friends carried me to a house where He was teaching. I was excited, not quite sure what to expect, but excited all the same. When we arrived, they found it was impossible to push through the crowd that surrounded Jesus. I was bitterly disappointed and I felt sorry for my friends who had gone to so much trouble, it seemed, for nothing. Then they came up with the bright idea of tearing a huge hole in the roof and lowering me down into the house. My emotions had gone haywire by that time.

(Pauses to reflect. Smiles.) Down I went, anticipating the reaction of an irate homeowner—unhappy with the recent "remodeling" job performed on his roof. But instead, there I was gazing into the face of Jesus and hearing Him say, "Son, your sins are forgiven." I felt as though a heavy, dark cloud just lifted from me.

The sensation was so strong I looked to see if my friends had started pulling me back up. I was startled when I realized I had not moved. So when Jesus told me to get up, pick up my bed, and go home, I felt so light, I didn't even question His command. I jumped, I walked, I ran, I danced, and I praised God every step of the way—for the forgiveness of sin, for my healing, and for Jesus.

What a blessing to have friends who will stop at nothing to be sure you have the opportunity to meet Jesus! *(Returns to seat.)*

MARY, JESUS' MOTHER *(walking to front, very emotional):* It seems like only yesterday that I experienced the thrill of holding my firstborn son. As I touched those tiny little hands, I was overwhelmed with awe. I stared at the innocent face of my precious newborn baby and whispered, with a heart full of wonder, "You are the promised Messiah!"

Then a few days later, when we took Him to the temple for dedication; I was puzzled when Simeon blessed Jesus, but warned me, "A sword shall pierce through your heart."

(Pause, as if deciding how to continue.) I recall the fear that flashed over me one particular day when we realized Jesus was not with our company returning from the Passover. After all, He was only twelve at the time. Joseph and I couldn't understand the urgency He felt to be about His Father's business.

Oh, I was so proud of Him the day I dared to believe that He could turn the water into wine during our friends' wedding feast at Cana of Galilee. This was only the beginning of countless miracles.

(Continues.) I also remember how it felt—how much it hurt—the day I stood outside where He was teaching a very large crowd. When the word finally reached Him that I wanted to see Him, He said, "Who is my mother?" Then He looked at the crowd and told them, "Whosoever shall do the will of God, the same is my brother and my sister and my mother."

But the pain I felt then was nothing compared to the agony I felt when I stood at the foot of the cross and looked up at His torn, blood-soaked body. I stared at the innocent, barely recognizable face of my son and whispered, "You were the promised Messiah!" *(Pauses.)* Then I realized, Simeon's prophecy had come true—A sword had pierced my heart! *(John comes forward to comfort Mary and assist her to her seat.)*

LUKE *(walking to front, incredulous and distraught):* Jesus did not have to die! Think about it!

The Scribes and the Pharisees followed Him around constantly. They recognized His wisdom and power, but they questioned His methods and authority. They tried to provoke Jesus into saying anything that they could use against Him. He wasn't afraid of them. In the face of their criticism and accusations, Jesus was never caught off guard. He knew exactly what they were thinking

and He knew what Judas was planning. He had repeatedly es-
caped arrest. He hid when they tried to stone Him. *(Snorts.)* Why
He walked right through their midst when they took Him out to
throw Him off of a hilltop. *(Pause, continues slowly.)* So, why was
this time different?

I don't believe anyone could have made Jesus do anything He
did not want to do. *(Pause, continues forcefully.)* Why? *(Looks up.
Continues perplexed and somewhat angrily.)* God, why? *(Pauses.)* Why
did You let them kill Your Son? *(Returns to seat dejectedly.)*

BOY *(walking to front, speaking brightly)*: I just wanted to say I sure
won't forget Jesus. Once you've met Him, you will never forget Him.

I had heard about Him doin' all kinds of miracle stuff, so I
decided to just go along and see for myself what was really
happenin'. I sorta thought He was some kind of magician or
somethin'. *(Shrugs shoulders.)* Well anyway, to make a long story
short, I guess I was the only person out of five thousand men
smart enough to take my lunch. *(Pauses.)* Andrew came to me and
asked me if I would be willing to share it. Sure was hard to give it
up. *(Sheepishly.)* After all, I'm just a growing boy. *(Pauses.)* But
Jesus took that lunch, blessed it, and turned five loaves and two
fishes into a feast.

I got to see a miracle firsthand! Even got to help a little. Looks to
me as though He went to a lot of trouble to feed all those people
when He could have just sent them home. But He really cared!
(Frowns, puzzled.) Wonder how come nobody cared for Him?
(Returns to seat.)

WOMAN HEALED OF THE ISSUE OF BLOOD *(walking to front, speaks with a
matter-of-fact tone)*: The doctors had finally given up on me. I had
been sick for years. Spent all the money I had trying to find a cure,
but I just got sicker and weaker. Then I heard about Jesus. He was
my last chance—my only hope. I had to reach Him—to reach out
and touch Him.

I could barely move. My voice was just a hoarse whisper. I
thought, no use to call out, He can't hear me. But with the last bit
of strength I had, so painfully, so slowly, I merely brushed the hem
of His garment. Healing power surged through my body instantly,
and I knew I was healed. One touch! One moment you are overwhelmed and going down for the last time—then you just reach
out and touch Jesus, and miraculously your whole life is changed!
(All murmur and nod while woman is returning to seat.)

ZACCHAEUS *(walks slowly to the front of room, clears throat, pauses, appears unsure how to begin):* I was literally up a tree the day I first saw Jesus. He looked up into that old sycamore tree and said, "Zacchaeus, come on down; I'm going home with you."

I went up that tree, a curious little man. I came down, feeling like a giant. Jesus entered my home that day. But more importantly, He entered my heart. *(Pauses.)* Seems like my story begins and ends with a tree. *(Pauses, then continues very slowly, thoughtfully.)* Once upon a time, I watched Jesus from a tree. *(Pauses.)* At the end, I watched Him die upon a tree. Jesus, the friend of publicans and sinners. My Friend! *(Returns to seat.)*

MATTHEW *(walking to front):* "Follow me."—Just two simple words spoken by Jesus to me as He passed by where I was sitting at the tax tables, and I felt compelled to obey His invitation immediately.

Oh, how marvelous the memories! *(With admiration.)* I heard the Sermon on the Mount. I saw the blind receive their sight, the lame walk, lepers cleansed, the deaf hear, the dumb talk, the dead raised, and those who were demon-possessed delivered. I was there when He rebuked the winds and calmed the sea!

I really enjoyed the times when He would take us aside and explain some of the parables He told so well. He even took the time to teach us how to pray.

I remember the turmoil that churned within me, during the Last Supper, when He said one of us would betray Him. He didn't answer when I asked, "Lord, is it I?"

Then later, I saw Him taken away from the Garden of Gethsemane. *(Appears to be too upset to speak anymore and returns to seat.)*

JAIRUS'S DAUGHTER *(walks to front, shyly):* I walked here today only because of Jesus. Don't get me wrong; I wasn't crippled. *(Pauses.)* I better start at the beginning.

(Pause, as though organizing thoughts.) Once, I was very, very sick. My father, Jairus, had heard about this Jesus who was going around healing people. So he searched until he found Jesus, then asked Him to come and heal me. While they were on the way to our house, some people went to tell my father not to "trouble the Master" anymore because I was already dead. But Jesus told him, "Be not afraid, only believe."

When they came to our house, my parents tell me, people laughed at Jesus because He said that I was only sleeping. I awakened from the dead when He said, "Maid, arise."

This is the first time I have ever told this story because only three of His disciples, my parents, and I were in that room, and He asked all of us to keep it a secret. Now that He's dead, I guess it's okay to talk about it. I think He would tell me it doesn't matter anymore.

I wish He could have lived until I was grown up. I had planned to thank Him again someday. Since that won't be possible, I at least wanted to come here and let all of you know what this wonderful man called Jesus had done for me.

(Pause reflectively.) You know, until that day I thought my father could do just about anything. Then I was sure Jesus could do anything. *(Pauses.)* Until now!

(Slowly, reflectively.) I am so confused. *(Returns to seat.)*

PHILIP *(walking to front, examining the people, then nodding head knowingly):* Withering branches.—That's what we are now. On one occasion, Jesus told us, "I am the true vine—dwell in Me and I will dwell in you. I am the vine, you are the branches. Whoever lives in me and I in him bears much fruit. However, apart from me you can do nothing."

(Sadly.) Here we are—"broken branches." And without the life of the Vine, we have already begun to wither.

(Shrugs and sighs.) Who knows what is going to happen to us now—what dreadful things we may have to face next? *(Confidently.)* Regardless of what tomorrow brings, I will never regret having been a disciple of this Jesus of Nazareth. Having seen and heard and tasted and felt things that most people have only dreamed about, because He called us.

Our time together has been all too short, but every moment is precious *(Pauses, continues with assurance.)* when it is spent in His presence. *(Returns to seat.)*

THOMAS *(walking to front, speaking forcefully):* There are hundreds—no, thousands of beautiful memories. But that's all they are, just memories. I know you shouldn't speak ill of the dead, but I've got to say what I'm positive we've all been thinking. How utterly embarrassing that one of us, a chosen apostle, should sell Jesus out—lead the soldiers right to Him. And He knew it! Jesus knew it! He told us at the Last Supper that one of us would betray HIM. I wonder why He let Judas do that to Him? And to us? What about us? Where is this kingdom He promised us? *(Shakes head. Looks at floor. Pauses. Continues angrily.)*

We trusted You, Jesus! We gave up an awful lot to follow You. And look where it got us.

Here we are. *(Looks up and gestures over crowd.)* Scared, hiding, don't know where to turn—what to do. *(Pauses. Continues brokenly, with eyes closed.)* We needed You, Jesus! We still need You! *(Returns to seat.)*

NICODEMUS *(walking to front, manner and speech authoritative):* "As Moses lifted up the serpent in the wilderness, even so must the Son of man be lifted up: that whosoever believeth in him should not perish, but have eternal life." He spoke those words to me one night. I have meditated often on "being born again of the Spirit" and "the light of the truth." All of His teaching just keeps spinning around in my head. I clearly remember His saying that He had told us earthly things and we didn't believe Him, so how could we believe if He told us about heavenly things. Then He added, "The Son of man came down from heaven." *(Pause and consider, rub chin, repeat slowly.)*

"The Son of man came down from heaven." *(Pauses.)* "The Son of man must be lifted up."

Could it be that we have seen the Son of man lifted up?

I don't know about all of you, but I believe. *(Emphatically, nodding head.)* Yes, I believe Jesus was the Son of God! *(Returns to seat.)*

MARY MAGDALENE *(Positions self inconspicuously behind a door that opens into the room where the memorial service is in progress and remains hidden until after the last character has finished speaking. Knocking loudly on door and yelling.):* Let me in! Let me in! It's Mary! Hurry! Let me in! *(Continues to knock and yell until the door is answered by Peter. Runs into room. Speaking to all, but darting from one to another, touching some of the characters. Joyously, with great excitement and eager to share the good news.)* He's alive! He's alive! I saw Him in the garden outside the tomb. I went to the tomb early this morning and the stone had been rolled away. There were angels inside! They said, "Don't weep, He is risen."

Then I saw Him in the garden. At first, I thought He was a gardener. Then He quietly spoke my name. And I knew it was Jesus! He told me to run and tell you the good news. He's not dead!!! He's alive!!!

16

(When Mary Magdalene knocks at the door, all characters jump up from seats and whisper to each other in a frightened manner. Finally, Peter will reluctantly and cautiously open the door. As Mary Magdalene begins speaking, all murmur with obvious disbelief. As she continues they become quiet and incredulous. After she finishes, all become noisy and jubilant, repeating to each other.)

ALL CHARACTERS: He's alive! He's alive! He's alive!

Optional ending: *(Narrator walks to front and faces audience.)*
NARRATOR: After the initial excitement diminished about the good news that Jesus had somehow conquered death, hell, and the grave, the disciples once again allowed doubt and fear to overcome them. But Jesus walked with them along the road, ate with them, appeared among them in locked rooms, even cooked their breakfast on the seashore. He explained that the many things written about Him in the law of Moses, by the prophets, and in the Psalms had to be fulfilled. And *(Emphatically.)* finally, *(Pauses.)* they understood!

They watched as He ascended into Heaven and were assured by the angels that someday He would return again. In obedience to their beloved Savior, they tarried in the Upper Room until the Holy Ghost came on the Day of Pentecost. Filled with His power, they began to tell everyone, "God so loved the world, that he gave his only begotten Son, that whosoever believeth in him . . . might be saved" (John 3:16-17 KJV). Some of the apostles shared the gospel with us *(Pauses and holds up a Bible.)* by writing about Jesus—In Loving Memory.

Suggested order of characters and suggested music:

Narrator—Introduction
James
John
   "Oh, How He Loves You and Me" by Kurt Kaiser *(change loves to loved)*
   "He Loved Me to Death" by Dottie Rambo and Dony McGuire
The Delivered Son
   "When Jesus Passed By" by Jeff Gibson *(change words to past tense)*
Simon Peter's Mother-in-law
Simon Peter
   "Who Put the Tears" by Carol Bass
Adulterous Woman
   "Calvary" by Dallas Holm

"I Should Have Been Crucified" by Gordon Jensen

"Go Ahead and Throw" by Randy Swift

Nathanael

"Ten Thousand Angels Cried" by David Patillo

Child

"In His Time" by Diane Ball

Martha

"He's Still Workin' On Me" by Joel Hemphill

Mary, Lazarus's Sister

"Broken and Spilled Out" by Gloria Gaither and Bill George (verses 1, 3 and chorus)

Lazarus

"His Name Is Life" by Carman

"The Day He Wore My Crown" by Phil Johnson (verses 1 and 2)

Paralytic Man

"No One Ever Cared For Me Like Jesus" by Charles F. Weigle (verses 1 and 2 and chorus)

"Yeshua Ha Mashiach" by Greg Davis and Greg Fisher

Mary, Jesus' mother

"Driving Nails" by Bruce Carroll, Mikey Hitch, and Kevin Thomas

"Tears Are a Language (God Understands)" by Gordon Jensen

Luke

"If That Isn't Love" by Dottie Rambo

"Walking My Lord Up Calvary's Hill" by Ruby Moody (verse 1 and chorus)

Boy

"Nobody Cared" by Jack Hayford

Woman healed of the issue of blood

"Garment of the Savior" by Kirk Talley and Tim Greene

Zacchaeus

"He Grew the Tree" by Chuck Lawrence

Matthew

Jairus's Daughter

"So Much to Thank Him For" by Robert Deel

"I Am the God That Healeth Thee" by Don Moen Philip

"Love Bigger Than Heaven" by Chris White

"When He Was on the Cross (I Was on His Mind)" by Ronnie Hinson and Mike Payne

"He Thought of Me" by Ronnie Hinson and Mitch Hunter Thomas

"Do I Trust You" by Twila Paris

Nicodemus

"The Hammer" by Ray Boltz

Mary Magdalene

"He Came Up" by Ernie Haase

"Meanwhile in the Garden" by Tina Sadler

"Alive, Alive, Alive Forevermore"

"He's Alive" by Don Francisco

"Out of the Grave" by Tim Greene

"Paid in Full" by Mitch Hunter

Narrator or Pastor—Optional Ending

"Because He Lives" by William J. and Gloria Gaither

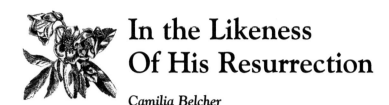

In the Likeness Of His Resurrection

Camilia Belcher

This is a dramatic recitation presented in verse, Scripture, and song, requiring at least one speaker *(four speakers [Disciples] are preferred).*

Prologue, Scenes 1 and 2, and Epilogue—In front of the congregation

Props: Each speaker has a Bible *(New International Version).*
Also required: Hymnals containing the following songs:
"Christ the Lord Is Risen Today" by Charles Wesley;
"Christ Arose!" by Robert Lowry;
"There Is a Fountain" by William Cowper;
"Rock of Ages" by Augustus M. Toplady/Thomas Hastings.

Time: First century A.D.

Scripture taken from the *New International Version.*

Prologue: The Awakening

The congregation sings the first, second, and third verses of "Christ the Lord Is Risen Today." When the song ends, the First Disciple rises, stands in front of the congregation, and begins speaking.

FIRST DISCIPLE: Christ "will awaken the dawn"!*

First light—
after a long, dark night
when He was buried deep in the earth,
encased in stone.
The Savior had suffered all alone,
feeling laden with the world's sins,
but aware of His own righteousness' worth.
Now, the morning has come.
Pale eyelids flutter

as His heart begins to beat again.
Gone is all the pain
tearing His feet and hands.
Miraculously, He leaves a tomb that is sealed.
Like after opening a window's shutter,
daylight floods in again,
into the morning that He stilled
by His awakening.

Joyful, He rises, free of the grave clothes
and of the cloth that bound His head.
Dawn awakens to the joy of His soul.
He is risen! He has risen from His bed!

"I am the Living One," He later says;
"I was dead,
and behold I am alive for ever and ever!
And I hold the keys of death and Hades" (Revelation 1:18).

No more shall the shadow of sin separate us
from Him; no more shall our sin
separate us and Him from the Father.

Outside the tomb,
He greets the rising sun.
The Son has risen! No more shall earth
encompass His form.
God's Holy One shall never see decay,
for He has won the victory over death.
By the Spirit, God has raised Him today.

One day, we, too, shall rise to greet the Son—
Our Morning star, our dawn.

(The First Disciple sits down at the prologue's end. Then the congrega-
tion sings the first and second verses, and the refrain of "Christ Arose."
When the song ends, the Second, Third, and Fourth Disciples rise from
their seats, stand in front of the congregation, and begin speaking.)

Scene 1: The Plan of Salvation

SECOND DISCIPLE: After Jesus rose from the dead and was with His disciples, "He said to them, 'This is what I told you while I was still with you: Everything must be fulfilled that is written about me in the Law of Moses, the Prophets and the Psalms'" (Luke 24:44).

THIRD DISCIPLE: "Then he opened their minds so they could understand the Scriptures" (Luke 24:45).

SECOND DISCIPLE: "He told them, 'This is what is written: The Christ will suffer and rise from the dead on the third day, and repentance and forgiveness of sins will be preached in his name to all nations, beginning at Jerusalem'" (Luke 24:46, 47).

FOURTH DISCIPLE: "Men of Israel, listen to this: Jesus of Nazareth was a man accredited by God to you by miracles, wonders and signs, which God did among you through him, as you yourselves know. This man was handed over to you by God's set purpose and foreknowledge; and you, with the help of wicked men, put him to death by nailing him to the cross. But God raised him from the dead, freeing him from the agony of death, because it was impossible for death to keep its hold on him" (Acts 2:22-24).

THIRD DISCIPLE: "When the people heard this, they were cut to the heart and said to Peter and the other apostles, 'Brothers, what shall we do?'" (Acts 2:37).

FOURTH DISCIPLE: "Peter replied, 'Repent and be baptized, every one of you, in the name of Jesus Christ for the forgiveness of your sins. And you will receive the gift of the Holy Spirit'" (Acts 2:38).

(The Disciples lead the congregation in singing the first verse of "There Is a Fountain." The Disciples continue speaking when the song ends.)

Scene 2: "That is written about me in the Law of Moses, the Prophets and the Psalms" (Luke 24:44).

THIRD DISCIPLE: "On the last and greatest day of the Feast, Jesus stood and said in a loud voice, 'If anyone is thirsty, let him come to me and drink. Whoever believes in me, as the Scripture has said, streams of living water will flow from within him!' By this he meant the Spirit, whom those who believed in him were later to receive. Up to that time the Spirit had not been given, since Jesus had not yet been glorified" (John 7:37-39).

FOURTH DISCIPLE: It was written of Christ in the law of Moses that

God's people "drank the same spiritual drink; for they drank from the spiritual rock that accompanied them, and that rock was Christ" (1 Corinthians 10:4).

SECOND DISCIPLE: When Israel was in the desert, Moses struck a
  rock, and out flowed water
to quench the people's thirst. Later,
God gave a river flowing through Christ.
Blood and water streamed out of Jesus' side
When He was crucified.

The Rock is Christ. He died
so that we might live,
our thirst for God's companionship
satisfied; our sins baptized
by the cover of His cleansing flood.

(The Disciples lead the congregation in singing 1—the first and third verses of "Rock of Ages." The verses that begin: "Rock of Ages, cleft for me"; and "Nothing in my hand I bring"; and then 2—the verse of "There Is a Fountain" that begins: "E'er since, by faith, I saw the stream Thy flowing wounds supply." The Disciples continue speaking when the song ends.)

THIRD DISCIPLE: "David said about him: 'I saw the Lord always before me. Because he is at my right hand, I will not be shaken. Therefore my heart is glad and my tongue rejoices; my body also will live in hope, because you will not abandon me to the grave, nor will you let your Holy One see decay. You have made known to me the paths of life; you will fill me with joy in your presence'" (Acts 2:25-28).

FOURTH DISCIPLE: "Seeing what was ahead, he spoke of the resurrection of the Christ, that he was not abandoned to the grave, nor did his body see decay. God has raised this Jesus to life, and we are all witnesses of the fact" (Acts 2:31, 32).

SECOND DISCIPLE: Jesus himself said, "For as Jonah was three days and three nights in the belly of a hugh fish, so the Son of Man will be three days and three nights in the heart of the earth" (Matthew 12:40).

(The Disciples lead the congregation in singing the third verse and the refrain of "Christ Arose!" The verse that begins: "Death cannot keep his prey." The Disciples continue speaking when the song ends.)

THIRD DISCIPLE: Jesus once told His disciples: "I have a baptism to undergo, and how distressed I am until it is completed!" (Luke 12:50).

FOURTH DISCIPLE: "For Christ died for sins once for all, the righteous for the unrighteous, to bring you to God. He was put to death in the body but made alive by the Spirit, through whom also he went and preached to the spirits in prison who disobeyed long ago when God waited patiently in the days of Noah while the ark was being built. In it only a few people, eight in all, were saved through water, and this water symbolizes baptism that now saves you also—not the removal of dirt from the body but the pledge of a good conscience toward God. It saves you by the resurrection of Jesus Christ, who has gone into heaven and is at God's right hand—with angels, authorities and powers in submission to him" (1 Peter 3:18-22).

SECOND DISCIPLE: Noah and his people entered their boat
as water submerged the sin
on the earth down below.
But the ark rose,
triumphantly intact,
through the waves, and floated
to safe land, to start life over again.

THIRD DISCIPLE: Jesus, our Savior, when He was crucified,
felt like a weight of water
polluted with accumulated sins
was pressing Him into the mire.
He felt all God's waves
wash over Him
in the death of baptism.

FOURTH DISCIPLE: Buried deep in the earth,
He rose to new life—
just as Noah's ark ended the search
for dry land, and those inside
rested securely on a mountaintop, high
above the pollution of sin.

SECOND DISCIPLE: Now, we will stand on God's mountaintop
with Christ's cloak as our covering—
when Christ returns to rule the kingdom of God—
because Jesus was the ark
who saved us through water, dying
our death for us. I awaken
in His watery grave
that is my well of life.

There all God's waves
washed over Him, so that grace
could bring us safe
in Him, to His mountainside.

Epilogue: Our Awakening

THIRD DISCIPLE: "Or don't you know that all of us who were baptized into Christ Jesus were baptized into his death? We were
therefore buried with him through baptism into death in order
that, just as Christ was raised from the dead through the glory of
the Father, we too may live a new life" (Romans 6:3, 4).

FOURTH DISCIPLE: "But your dead will live; their bodies will rise. You
who dwell in the dust, wake up and shout for joy. Your dew is like
the dew of the morning; the earth will give birth to her dead"
(Isaiah 26:19).

SECOND, THIRD, AND FOURTH DISCIPLES: "If we have been united
with him like this in his death, we will certainly also be united
with him in his resurrection" (Romans 6:5).

*(The Disciples lead the congregation in singing the fourth verse of
"Christ the Lord Is Risen Today." The verse that begins: "Soar we now
where Christ has led.")*

*The quoted words are from Psalm 57:8.

Scripture References: Psalm 57:8; Isaiah 26:19; Matthew 12:40; Luke 12:50; Luke
24:44-47; John 7:37-39; Acts 2:22-28, 31, 32, 37, 38; Romans 6:3-5; 1 Corinthians 10:4;
1 Peter 3:18-22; Revelation 1:18.

Other Scripture References: Exodus 17:1-7; Psalm 16:8-11; Psalm 69 (cf. John 2:17;
Matthew 27:34; Romans 11:9, 10); Psalms 87:1; 88:6-9, 16, 17; 105:41; 108:1-5; 110:3;
Isaiah 2:2, 3; Jonah 2:1-6; Matthew 28:1-10; Mark 16:1-19; Luke 24:1-12; John 20:1-9;
1 Corinthians 15:12-57; Ephesians 5:14; Revelation 3:4, 5, 18; 19:7-9.

Reflections and Forgiveness

Iris Gray Dowling

Those who were near Jesus during His life, at His crucifixion, and resurrection meet to reflect on what happened. They accept God's forgiveness and realize a duty to tell others about Him.

Characters:
Mary and Joseph, parents of Jesus
Peter and John, disciples of Jesus
Basilio, a Roman soldier
Paolo, the Roman soldier's son
Joseph of Arimathea
People *(1 or 2) optional*
Bible Reader and/or Narrator
Singing Group *(choir or audience)*

Production Notes: This program can be produced on stage or as Reader's Theatre with name cards for character identity. *(Notes for stage production are included.)* Slides optional for some scenes: *(Pictures of Jesus' Nazareth home, stable, birth, crucifixion, and empty tomb.)* Singers can be choir, small groups, or audience. Certain stanzas of songs were chosen because of their message content. All Scriptures are from the *King James Version.*

Costumes: Traditional biblical costumes. In Reader's Theatre, use large name cards worn for identification.

Setting: Outside Mary and Joseph's home.

Scene 1

NARRATOR: This scene takes place in front of Jesus' boyhood home in Nazareth with Mary and Joseph talking.
Music: "Tell Me the Story of Jesus" *(Group sings stanza 1. Mary and Joseph enter SL during song. They talk quietly and carry board and carpenter's tools.)*

MARY *(looks at Joseph):* Joseph, I've wondered so many times why God chose us to be the earthly parents of His Son. We didn't have much of this world's goods to give Him. He deserved so much more.

JOSEPH *(holding his tools):* We do live in a small unknown village. I'm just a humble carpenter. I've never thought of being rich. I'm sure God knew all that.

MARY: I think of Gabriel's words to us, "Hail, thou that art highly favored, the Lord is with thee: blessed art thou among women. . . . Fear not, Mary: for thou hast found favor with God . . . Thou shalt . . . bring forth a son and shalt call His name JESUS. . . . for He shall save His people from their sins."

SINGING GROUP: "Thou Didst Leave Thy Throne" *(stanza 2)*

JOSEPH: It's a miracle how God cared for us on those trips—to Bethlehem and then Egypt. And His salvation plan took place without a mistake.

MARY: You know, Joseph, as I think about our simple home, I know God wanted Jesus to grow up here with us.

JOSEPH: What do you mean?

MARY: The Father in Heaven wanted Jesus to be humble and ready to meet all kinds of people, even the very poor.

JOSEPH: You always have a lot of insight, Mary. *(Pauses.)* Where is our boy, anyway?

MARY: He's at the back of the house teaching his friends God's ways.

JOSEPH: What a child! Let's go in for some food now. *(He takes Mary's hand. Exit SL taking props; lights down.)*

Transitional Music: "One Day!" *(Group sings stanzas 1, 2, and 4 with refrain following stanza 4 only. Optional slides of Nativity, crucifixion, empty tomb, and back to Nazareth home can be used at appropriate places in song.)*

Scene 2

NARRATOR: Jesus was born and died for our sins, but He arose from the dead and we know He's alive in Heaven today. Scene 2 takes place in front of Jesus' boyhood home ten years after His ascension. Peter came to see John and Mary. Peter and John are talking together. Basilio, Paolo, and two people stand at a distance and look at the home. *(Lights up.)*

(Peter enters SL carrying scroll; knocks, waits.)

JOHN *(sitting in chair, writing; looks up; greets Peter):* Peter, what brings you here?

PETER: I came to see you and Mary. I wondered how she's doing.

JOHN: She's been resting better lately. *(Points to Soldiers and People.)* Who are those people over there?

PETER: I think they want to see Jesus' boyhood home. Remember how we traveled with Jesus when He taught so many people. We watched Him heal the sick and raise people from the dead. There were some who believed, but others who criticized Him.

JOHN *(excited):* It's amazing how we walked with Him, probably no more than two hundred miles from Nazareth. We walked beside Him without realizing the privilege of being with God's Son.

PETER: I'm writing some stories about our experiences. Listen to this. *(Opens scroll; reads 2 Peter 1:17, 18.)* "He received from God the Father honor and glory, when there came such a voice to him from the excellent glory, This is my beloved Son, in whom I am well pleased. And this voice which came from heaven we heard, when we were with him in the holy mount."

JOHN: Yes, I remember. We heard God say several other times how pleased He was with His Son, Jesus.

PETER: Both of us were close disciples, but I can't believe I denied Him. How I must have grieved Him . . .

JOHN: Peter, Jesus forgave you. Now you tell people about Him as He wanted you to. *(Pauses, as he looks away.)* Look, that Roman soldier seems to be coming here.

PETER *(turns to Basilio as they walk closer from SR):* What brings you here?

BASILIO: I came to show my son the place where Jesus grew up. I want him to know more about Jesus than I did.

JOHN: This is only a simple house.

BASILIO: I couldn't help but hear what you said. *(Sad voice.)* I also need God's forgiveness. I hit this innocent man who did nothing wrong! I spat on Him. I put the crown of thorns on His head.

PAOLO: Didn't He fight back, Father?

BASILIO *(sorrowful voice):* No, He never even talked back. Pilate knew Jesus was innocent, too, but feared the loss of his job if he didn't go along with the crowd.

PAOLO: What did Pilate do, Father?

BASILIO: He let Jesus be crucified on the cross.

PAOLO: You said you helped put Him on the cross.

BASILIO *(sadly):* Yes. I don't like to think about it. He died like a criminal on a crude Roman cross. We soldiers gambled over His clothes. When I looked up at Jesus' bleeding body, I asked, "Why?"

PAOLO: Now you know, Father.

BASILIO *(wipes sweat from face):* Oh, yes . . . a little later, I learned Jesus died for sinners like me. Now I want to tell them about His innocence.

JOHN: Jesus forgave His enemies. All you need to do is believe and obey Jesus' commands and ask to be forgiven.

BASILIO: Yes, I have done that.

(Joseph of Arimathea knocks and enters from SR.)

PETER: Here comes our old friend, Joseph from Arimathea. *(Greets Joseph; speaks to soldiers and others.)* You remember, this is the man who asked Pilate for the body of Jesus.

JOSEPH OF A: Yes, I took Jesus down from the cross, carefully wrapped His body for burial, and put Him in my new tomb.

JOHN: We're glad you took care of Him.

JOSEPH A: Later, I found how I had fulfilled God's divine plan prophesied in Isaiah 53:9.

PAOLO: What does it say?

JOSEPH A: "He made his grave with the wicked, and with the rich in his death; because he had done no violence, neither was any deceit in his mouth."

JOHN *(points to Basilio):* And all your soldiers sealed the tomb tight.

BASILIO *(firmly):* We followed Pilate's orders to make sure no one stole Jesus' body. He didn't want people to say He rose from the dead.

PAOLO: But Jesus got out of that sealed tomb, anyway.

BASILIO: I know He arose. I heard a loud earthquake and then I couldn't wake up. That proves to me God had something to do with it.

JOHN *(talks toward Paolo):* You know, I'm writing several books about Jesus and His teachings. I wrote in the gospel of John that He rose from the dead and was seen by all of the disciples. We had no doubt after His resurrection that He was the same person who walked and talked with us.

PETER: I'm glad He appeared to us several times after His death. We saw His power firsthand. Now we know He can give eternal life as He promised.

JOHN *(looking at scroll):* Listen to what I wrote about Jesus teachings: "These things have I written unto you that believe on the name of the Son of God; that ye may know that ye have eternal life, and that ye may believe on the name of the Son of God. And this is the confidence that we have in him" (1 John 5:13, 14).

PETER *(points to scroll):* You made it clear, Jesus is really God. We can go to Heaven if we believe in Him.

JOHN: There's so much I want to tell about His works, but the world couldn't hold all the books that could be written.

ALL: That's certainly the truth.

BASILIO: Come on, Paolo. Now that we've seen Jesus' boyhood home, we need to go tell a lot of people more about Him, too.

PAOLO: I'm glad you brought me here, Father. *(Starts to walk SR with Basilio.)*

BASILIO: Yes, so am I. Now I know for sure Jesus forgave me of my sins. *(Basilio and Paolo exit SR; Lights down.)*

Music: "Tell Me the Story of Jesus" *(Group sings stanza 2, 3 and refrain. During song entire cast kneels—backs to audience, facing empty cross with light on it.)*

NARRATOR OR BIBLE READER *(reading Philippians 2:5-11):* "Christ Jesus, . . . being in the form of God, thought it not robbery to be equal with God: but made himself of no reputation, and took upon him the form of a servant, and was made in the likeness of men: and being found in fashion as a man, he humbled himself, and became obedient unto death, even the death of the cross. Wherefore God also hath highly exalted him, and given him a name which is above every name: that at the name of Jesus every knee should bow, of things in heaven, and things in the earth, and things under the earth; and that every tongue should confess that Jesus Christ is Lord, to the glory of God the Father."

Music: "O for a Thousand Tongues to Sing" *(Group sings all 5 stanzas. All continue to kneel during four stanzas. During stanza 5 the Characters all stand and turn toward audience.)*

ALL: "Thou Didst Leave Thy Throne" *(All cast, singers, and audience stand and sing stanza 5.)*

The Missing Egg

Dolores Steger

An Easter play in one act for older youth/teens, with small parts for younger children and adults.

Characters and Costumes:

Five older youth/teens, dressed casually

Any number of children, dressed casually, eleven with small speaking parts

Any number of Adults/Older Youth/Teens to portray mothers/fathers, dressed casually, nonspeaking parts

Props—Required

Two Easter baskets with six plastic eggs in one and five plastic eggs in the other

Twelve wrapped prize packages, one containing a cross large enough to be seen by audience when held up. *(Note: the package with the cross should be clearly marked so it is not "given out" to one of the children during the play's action.)*

Large sign reading "Easter Egg Hunt Here! Find an Egg and Get a Prize!"

Chair or bench; Easter grass; palm frond, real or made from construction paper; loaf of bread *(empty bread wrapper stuffed with newspaper may be used)*; crown, made from yellow/gold foil paper; adult-size night robe/bathrobe; cane with curved handle to look like shepherd's crook/staff; wristwatch for Teen 2

Props—Optional

Backdrop/frieze of trees, shrubs, flowers, painted on craft paper; benches; chairs; round garbage cans; any other park setting items

Time: The present

Place: A park

Music: Tape/Choir/Piano/Organ

Setting: Stage is set to look like a park; Easter grass is scattered about; sign is placed front stage left; chair/bench for prizes is placed front stage right; palm frond, bread, cane, robe, crown are placed in various places on stage but hidden from audience view by Easter grass or other objects.

Music plays "In the Garden." Teens enter rear stage right, two of them carrying baskets with eggs, the rest carrying prize packages; they move to front center stage and Teen 4 speaks when music ends.

TEEN 4 *(pointing to chair/bench):* Let's put the prizes here.

OTHERS: Okay.

TEEN 1 *(to Teen 2):* What time is it?

TEEN 2 *(looking at watch):* We've still got some time before the kids arrive.

TEEN 1: Good. Is anyone around?

(Teens look around.)

TEEN 3: No. It's safe!

TEEN 1: Then let's start hiding the eggs.

TEEN 5: Remember not to make them too difficult to find. Little kids will be looking for them and we want the eggs to be found.

OTHERS: Right.

TEEN 4: And try to remember where you hide them in case we have to help the kids find them.

OTHERS: Right!

TEEN 3: Let's go.

(Teens hide eggs in various places on stage then move near bench with prizes; empty baskets are placed on floor near bench.)

TEEN 2: That does it.

TEEN 3 *(pointing rear stage left):* Just in time, too! Here they come now!

(Children and "parents" enter rear stage left and move to center stage; when all are there, Teen 1 speaks.)

TEEN 1 *(to children and parents):* Thanks for coming to our Easter Egg Hunt. We hope you find the eggs we've hidden.

TEEN 2: Before we begin the hunt, we'd like to tell you the rules. *(Pause.)* The eggs are hidden in this part of the park only. *(Teen points around stage.)* Each egg is worth a prize. When you find an egg, bring it to us at this bench. *(Pointing to chair/bench where prize packages have been placed.)* Then we'll give you a prize. When we call "time's up" everyone must stop hunting.

TEEN 3: One last rule. This egg hunt is for children only. Adults, please don't help them.

TEEN 4: Are there any questions? *(Children, parents shake heads no.)* Then, on your mark, get set, go!

(Adults move to rear stage left; teens stay by chair/bench with prizes; children scatter to look for eggs; music plays two verses of "All Things Bright and Beautiful" as children search; Child 1 speaks when music stops.)

CHILD 1 *(excitedly):* I found one! I found one! *(Child rushes to bench to collect prize.)*

TEEN 5 *(taking egg from child and placing it in basket, then handing prize to child):* Here's your prize! Happy Easter!

CHILD 1 *(rushing off to parent):* Look what I got!

(Note: When children go to parents, parents express joy by patting them on the back, clapping, hugging them, etc. Child 1 returns to hunt, leaving prize with parent.)

CHILD 2: Here's one! Here's one! I've got one!

CHILD 3: Me, too! Me, too!

(Child 2 and 3 rush to bench for prizes and exchange eggs for prizes as before.)

TEEN 5 *(handing out prizes):* Congratulations and happy Easter!

CHILD 2 AND 3 *(rushing to parents):* Look! Look! A prize!

(Child 2 and 3 leave prizes with parents and return to hunt as before.)

CHILD 4: I think I found one! I did! I did!

CHILD 5: And here's another!

(Child 4 and 5 rush to exchange eggs for prizes as before.)

TEEN 5 *(handing out prizes):* Good job and happy Easter!

CHILD 4 AND 5 *(rushing to parents):* Hooray! Hooray! We've found some eggs.

(Child 4 and 5 return to hunt as before.)

CHILD 6: Here's an egg!

CHILD 7: And here's one, too!

CHILD 8: And here's another. Let's get our prizes!

(Child 6, 7, 8 exchange eggs for prizes as before.)

TEEN 5 *(handing out prizes):* Here's your prize—and yours—and yours. Happy Easter!

(Child 6, 7, 8 rush to parents.)

CHILD 6, 7, 8: Look! Look! Look what we got!

(Child 6, 7, 8 return to hunt.)

CHILD 9: See! Here! Here's one!

CHILD 10: Here's one, too!

CHILD 11: And here's one for me!

(Child 9, 10, 11 exchange eggs for prizes as before.)

TEEN 5 *(handing out prizes):* Happy Easter to you all!

(Child 9, 10, 11 rush to parents.)

CHILD 9, 10, 11: We found some! We found some!

(Child 9, 10, 11 stay by parents as Teen 1 calls out.)

TEEN 1: Time's up.

(Children stop hunting and go to parents at rear stage left; Teen 2 speaks when all are there.)

32

Teen 2: Thanks for coming to our Easter Egg Hunt. We hope you had a good time.

(Parents and children clap.)

Teen 3: Before you leave we want to wish each and every one of you a very happy Easter!

(Parents and children clap again and leave rear stage left; teens watch them leave; Teen 4 speaks when all have left.)

Teen 4: Well. That was a success.

Teen 5: Even better than last year.

Teen 1: Now for the cleanup. We can't leave this place in a mess or they won't let us come back next year.

Teen 2 *(looking at bench where one prize remains):* That's strange!

Others: What?

Teen 2: There's one prize left.

Teen 3: That means there's an egg still hidden somewhere.

Teen 1: Do you think we called time too soon?

Teen 4: No! We gave the kids plenty of time!

Teen 5: Oh, well, we'll just look for the missing egg while we're cleaning up. One of us is sure to find it.

Others: Yeah!

(Teens scatter for cleanup and search for missing egg; music plays 1 verse of "In the Garden." Teen 1 speaks when music ends.)

Teen 1 *(bending and picking up loaf of bread):* Hey, you guys! *(Other teens stop what they're doing and look toward Teen 1.)* Look what I found. *(Holds up bread.)*

Teen 2: A loaf of bread. Who could've left that here?

Teen 3: Someone probably had a picnic and forgot about it. *(To Teen 1.)* Just put it on the bench with the leftover prize. We'll take care of it later.

(Teen 1 puts bread on bench; all teens continue cleanup/search; pause while searching, then Teen 2 speaks.)

Teen 2 *(bending and picking up crown):* Odd! Very odd!

(Other teens stop and look.)

Others: What?

Teen 2 *(holding up crown):* Look what I found! How did this get here?

Teen 4: Probably from the picnic. It must have been a birthday party or something and they left the bread and the crown behind. Put it with the bread for now.

(Teen 2 puts crown on bench; all continue cleanup; pause while searching, then Teen 3 speaks.)

Teen 3: Well, I never!

(Other teens stop searching and look at Teen 3 who is holding a palm frond.)

TEEN 5: It's a palm frond.

TEEN 3: I know that!

TEEN 5: So?

TEEN 3: Do you see any palm trees around here?

TEEN 5: Well, no.

TEEN 1: It has to have come from somewhere. It didn't just blow in!!

TEEN 2: Probably from an Easter program someone put on.

TEEN 4: In the park?

TEEN 2: Sure! Why not?

TEEN 4: If I were putting on an Easter program I wouldn't have it in the park. What if it rained?

TEEN 3: I'll just put it on the bench with the other stuff. We can talk about where it came from later.

OTHERS: Good!

(Teen 3 puts frond on bench; all teens continue cleanup. Pause while searching, then Teen 4 speaks.)

TEEN 4: Oh-oh! Oh-oh!

(Teens stop and turn toward Teen 4.)

TEEN 1: What now?

TEEN 4 *(holding up cane/crook)*: Take a look at this!

TEEN 2: It's a cane!

TEEN 3: Must have been left by someone at that picnic or birthday party or whatever.

TEEN 1: It kind of looks like a shepherd's crook.

TEEN 5: I don't think there are many shepherds around here, do you?

TEEN 4: If you used a cane, would you just leave it behind and forget it? Tell me. Would you?

TEEN 3: Well, I guess not, but—

TEEN 4 *(interrupting):* I'll put it on the bench with the other stuff. Maybe, later, we can trace its owner somehow.

(Teen 4 puts cane on bench; all continue cleanup. Pause, then Teen 5 speaks.)

TEEN 5: That does it!

(Others stop and look at Teen 5 who is holding up a robe.)

TEEN 5: Would you believe someone left this robe in the park?

TEEN 1: It looks a little worn but not bad enough to get rid of it.

TEEN 2: Put it with the other stuff.

(Teen 5 puts robe on bench; all continue cleanup. Pause, then Teen 3 speaks.)

TEEN 3: The place looks pretty clean to me! I think we're done.

OTHERS: Yeah.

TEEN 4: We still haven't found the missing egg!

TEEN 1: No. But if we couldn't find it, I don't think anyone else will either. Let's give up.

OTHERS: Okay!

TEEN 2: Let's take a look at the stuff we picked up.

(Teens move to bench and pick up items they collected.)

TEEN 3: Sure is a wild assortment!

TEEN 4: Bread—palm frond—crown—cane, or crook, if you want to call it that—old robe! Different for sure!

TEEN 5: Not like the usual things you pick up after an Easter egg hunt.

TEEN 1: Not at all!

TEEN 2 *(thinking):* A shepherd's crook—a waving palm—a loaf of bread—a robe—a crown—a Savior!

OTHERS: A what?

TEEN 2: A Savior! Look at all of these things! Don't they somehow remind you of Jesus?

OTHERS: Well—

TEEN 1: What'll we do with all of it?

TEEN 3: Let's take it to the park office. They'll be able to find out who it belongs to better than we can.

TEEN 2 *(looking at bench):* Wait a minute! There's something on the bench.

OTHERS: Yeah!

TEEN 3: Oh, yeah! It's the unopened prize for the missing egg!

TEEN 4: Let's open it now! *(To Teen 5.)* Your mom picked out the prizes and wrapped them, so you get the honors. Go on and open it.

TEEN 5 *(picking up prize package):* My mother said she was wrapping small toys and games and crayons so it's probably something like that.

TEEN 1: Well, open it and let's find out!

(Teen 5 opens package and holds up cross.)

ALL: It's a cross!

TEEN 5: How could that have gotten there?

TEEN 1: Your mother must have run out of toys or whatever. She must have put it there!

TEEN 5: I don't think—

TEEN 2 *(interrupting):* Does anyone get the feeling someone is trying to send us a message?

OTHERS: Someone?

TEEN 2 *(looking up and pointing skyward):* Someone!

OTHERS: A message?

TEEN 3: A message? A message? What kind of message?

TEEN 4: Any ideas?

TEEN 1: Maybe it has something to do with the missing egg!

OTHERS: Like what?

TEEN 1: Maybe the message is that we shouldn't think so much about Easter Egg Hunts or missing eggs and think more about what Easter really means—that the Lord died for us—

TEEN 2 *(interrupting)*: And rose—

TEEN 3 *(interrupting)*: To be with us—

TEEN 4 *(interrupting)*: By our sides—

TEEN 5 *(interrupting)*: Always and forever!

ALL: Wow! He's alive! He lives!

TEEN 1: Let's not take these things to the park office! Let's take them with us and show them to our folks!

TEEN 2: Do you think they'll get the message?

OTHERS: For sure!

(Teens 1 and 2 pick up Easter baskets with eggs; teens start walking toward front stage left carrying items, including baskets.)

TEEN 3: There's just one thing that still puzzles me!

OTHERS: What's that?

TEEN 3: You know! The egg! The missing egg!

OTHERS: Yeah! The missing egg! Oh well!

(Music plays "He Lives." Youth/Teens start leaving front stage left; Teen 3 picks up egg hunt sign and leaves, all participants return for curtain call and speak, as music plays softly.)

ALL: Do **you** know where it is? Have **you** seen it? Have **you** seen the missing egg? *(Pause.)* Happy Easter!

No Parade Permit

V. Louise Cunningham

This could be split into two skits. One for Palm Sunday and one for Easter.

Characters
Modern Day: Joe, Fred, Gary
Temple Officials: John, Addi, Eran, Lemuel

Setting: A split stage can be used effectively for this production. There is a modern-day office with traffic control on one side and on the other side a temple office during the time of Jesus.

Props: Desks or tables, chairs, benches, scrolls

Time: Present with flashback to Bible times

Costumes: Modern dress and biblical style robes.

Scene 1—Modern Office

Joe, Fred and Gary are at their desks or sitting around a table.

JOE: I can't believe all the paperwork we generate in this office.
FRED: Just think of how much we contribute to the paper recycling plants.
JOE: I, for one, think all of this stuff is a waste of time and effort besides being frustration for all the people who have to come through our office. Take this case for example. Someone wants to have a block party and close off a couple block on their streets. Not only do we have to clear it in our office b then . . .
GARY: . . . It goes to crowd control to see if there need for police officers to direct traffic or in case things get too rowdy.
FRED: Then the garbage and litter people get into the act because there will be all that to clean up the next day.
JOE: It's too bad we don't live in a simpler day and age when people wanted to picnic together—they just did it.
GARY: It makes it hard to be spontaneous.
JOE: Wonder what it was like in Jesus' time.

Scene 2—Temple Office

John, Eran and Addi are present.

JOHN: I, for one, will be glad when the Passover is over. We have so many out-of-town relatives staying with us.

ERAN: I know what you mean. People descend on us like a plague of locusts. My wife's sister and her family came. They have three teenage boys. They are about to eat us out of house and home.

JOHN: You look awful this morning. Did you have to wait for fresh bagels?

ADDI: Obviously you don't know what happened yesterday or you wouldn't care about bagels and lattes.

ERAN: What's going on?

JOHN: I was about to find out.

ADDI: I can't believe you didn't hear about the parade.

ERAN: There was no parade scheduled for Sunday. There weren't even any applications pending.

JOHN: Then that lets us off the hook. Who was it?

ADDI: Jesus and His disciples. Jesus rode a colt into town.

ERAN: So were there a lot of people around?

ADDI: The whole town practically, except for you two. At least it seemed that way with all the out-of-town people in for the Passover. As Jesus rode into town, the people were shouting "Hosanna to the King of David" and things like that.

JOHN: Only kings ride colts in our culture.

ERAN: And He didn't even have a permit.

ADDI: Even if He applied it wouldn't have been granted. It would have been shuffled from office to office and then misplaced. We've done that lots of times.

JOHN: Does anyone know His address? We will have to send Him a bill and a fine.

ADDI: I don't think He has one.

ERAN: He said one time something about foxes have holes, and birds have nests but He doesn't have any place to put His head.

ADDI: What about His friends in Bethany—Martha and Mary?

JOHN: If they are His friends, we are in big trouble. They have a brother Lazarus whom Jesus raised from the dead.

ERAN: I remember hearing about that.

JOHN: So let's go back to the parade. Do we need to send out a cleanup crew?

ADDI: I'd say so. People pulled branches off the palm trees and threw them in the road or else they put their cloaks on the ground for Jesus and His disciples to walk on.

JOHN: We could be in trouble when the temple officials hear about it. The first thing to do is contact the sanitation department.

ERAN: What a time for this to happen with all of the out-of-town people here. It really makes the temple people look bad.

ADDI: I hate to burst your bubble but things are worse than cleaning up the parade route. The sanitation men are a little busy in the temple courtyard.

ERAN: I noticed it was pretty messy this morning. What happened?

ADDI: I can't believe you haven't heard anything about this. After Jesus came into Jerusalem, He came storming into the courtyard and threw out the money changers again.

JOHN: I remember the mess from the last time Jesus did that. We still need to get workers out to clean up the parade route, though.

ERAN: It's not going to be easy with so many people on vacation because of the Passover. They'll have to be called back in.

ADDI: They sure won't like that. Maybe overtime will help ease things.

JOHN: The general public won't like it either. With all the carts picking up branches and things, there will be traffic jams.

ERAN: Unfortunately, it can't be helped.

JOHN: Oh, boy, we are going to be in trouble. I see where we have a real problem.

ADDI: You said it. Look who's coming.

LEMUEL *(enters):* You're all to report to Heber's office immediately! *(Exits.)*

JOHN: I'm not surprised we're summoned to the chief's office.

ERAN: I suggest we start working on our resumes.

JOHN: Maybe we can work this to our advantage. The Jews want to kill Jesus anyhow. This gives them more reason to be upset with Him, not us.

ADDI: You have a point there. Let's think ahead. It's common knowledge they want to get rid of Jesus one way or another. If they can find some way to have Him crucified after the Passover, we can give them suggestions for the best route to use to Golgotha.

ERAN: That sounds like a good idea. What if they aren't planning on getting rid of Jesus that way?

JOHN: We could help them work it all out. You know, give suggestions.

ADDI: Maybe we can find a way to pull the fat out of the fire yet.

ERAN: Gird your loins; I can hear our boss exploding from here.

Scene 3—Modern Office

Fred, Joe and Gary are present.

FRED: Hey, Joe, are you with us? You look like you are a hundred miles away.

JOE: More like 2000 years away.

GARY: Would you care to elaborate?

JOE: I was just thinking what it would have been like to be an official during the time of Jesus. When He had His triumphal entrance into Jerusalem, He just did it.

FRED: As I recall, it was a spur-of-the-moment thing. He didn't have to go through the hassles we do.

GARY: He also didn't have to be sure He didn't hurt anyone's feelings by not letting them march in His parade. There are so many groups now that feel they must be included in everything, even if it has nothing to do with them.

JOE: They are the first ones to go to the ACLU with lawsuits. Here's an example.

Scene 4—Modern Office

A week later, Joe, Gary and Fred are at work.

GARY: Time for a coffee break.

FRED: I think it's past time for a break. What a day.

JOE: Can you imagine what it was like in New York?

GARY: Oh yes, the famous Easter Parade. Why do you think it got started?

FRED: So the ladies could show off their spring clothes.

JOE: I'm glad our town doesn't have one. I was just thinking.

GARY: Oh no, hang onto your hats.

FRED: Easter bonnets you mean.

JOE: Can you imagine what it would have been like in the temple office if Jesus decided to have another parade after He was resurrected?

GARY: He could have had all the people who were raised from the dead when He was crucified.

FRED: That would sure shake up some people. Imagine some old reprobate prancing around, his family thinking they were well rid of him.

JOE: I remember hearing it read during a Good Friday service that the bodies of many holy people were brought back to life—not the bad ones.

GARY: So you're saying Jesus could have walked or rode a colt back into Jerusalem, followed by the people raised from the dead, and His disciples and followers. That would have given some of the timid believers enough courage to join in.

FRED: What an impact that would have had on the temple officials. Imagine how dismayed they would have been.

JOE: I think a stronger word than dismayed could be used. I think it was bad enough for them anyhow when the guards came in and said the body was missing.

Scene 5—Temple Office

John, Addi and Eran are at work. All look exhausted.

JOHN: This has certainly been a week.

ADDI: And I thought we had problems with Jesus not having a parade permit.

ERAN: This sure makes that look like small potatoes.

JOHN: At least for once, this isn't our problem. We had things all worked out with all our departments for the march to Golgotha.

ADDI: I think there will be an investigation into all that went on this week. If not, there should be.

ERAN: Did you get in on any of the meetings where they tried to find two witnesses to testify against Jesus?

JOHN: The officials certainly had egg all over their faces during that episode.

ADDI: That's not all. Those night meetings weren't legal, and they knew that.

ERAN: All they could think of was to get everything neatly tied up and taken care of before the Passover.

JOHN: Now all we have to worry about is a man like Barabbas being let go.

ADDI: People are so funny. Why didn't they shout out to have Jesus released?

JOHN: They did. But if you noticed the whole crowd was planted with men from the temple. It was all staged.

ERAN: Pilate turned out to be a wimp. He didn't have the guts to stop the farce. It looked as though he were going to until the Jews threatened him with going to Caesar.

ADDI: It's all over with now.

JOHN: Then why are some of the officials running around the temple?
(Lemuel enters.)
JOHN: So what's happening, Lemuel?
LEMUEL: You'll be hearing soon enough. The higher up muck-a-mucks are looking for ready money and may raid your petty cash if they get desperate enough.
ADDI: They won't find much here because of downsizing and cutbacks in our department. After that big cleanup of the temple and the highway, we're about tapped out.
ERAN: What do they need it for?
LEMUEL: You're up to speed on the crucifixion of Jesus, right?
JOHN: Yes. He died on the cross and Joseph of the Sanhedrin and Nicodemus took the body and put it in a tomb.
ADDI: I heard the higher-ups had the Romans post a guard for the tomb so the disciples wouldn't steal the body and say Jesus was resurrected.
LEMUEL: The guards were at the tomb. There was an earthquake, and the guards said they saw an angel. The men said they shook and couldn't do anything. Then when they looked, the body of Jesus was gone. The first thing they did was run over there to tell the high priest.
ERAN: Who took the body?
LEMUEL: No one knows. The guards swear they didn't sleep all night. They probably didn't because if they didn't stay awake on guard duty, they know they would be killed.
JOHN: It sure sounds strange. Jesus and others kept talking about His body being raised in three days. You don't suppose . . . ?
ADDI: All this stuff is messing with your mind. There is some logical explanation.
LEMUEL: You didn't hear it from me, but in the meantime the officials want to bribe the guards into saying they fell asleep.
JOHN: So they are paying them off?
ERAN: What a cover-up.
ADDI: I'm glad our office wasn't involved in any part of this.
LEMUEL: I better let the other people know what is going on. Rumors get started so easily.
ERAN: I think it is a lot of fuss about nothing. In a hundred years or less, nobody will care anything about all this!

Scene 6—Modern Office

Joe, Fred and Gary in office but on coffee break.

JOE: Time to go back to work.

FRED: Thanks, Joe.

JOE: You're welcome. For what?

FRED: You made me think about a different aspect of Easter and what Jesus went through.

GARY: We have all read or heard Bible stories since we were children, but thinking about the workers in the temple and seeing it from their viewpoint makes the Scriptures come alive. If we worked in the temple, would we have been any different?

JOE: We would like to think we would have been outspoken believers.

FRED: I guess what is more important is what are we going to do about what we know today? Imagine them trying to cover-up the resurrection. How did they think they would get away with it?

GARY: The same way people try to today.

FRED: I wonder if they had to raid the petty cash.

The Truth of the Matter

Dolores Steger

Characters
Journalist
Secretary to Pilate
Mary Magdalene
Peter
Aide to Caiaphas
Thomas

Place: A road near Jerusalem

Time: Two months after Jesus' resurrection

Scenery—Optional: bulletin board paper/carpeting to indicate a roadway, spread diagonally from rear stage left to front stage right; artificial plants/shrubs, or plants/shrubs painted on cartons, placed along path; bench

Props: Paper rolled to resemble a scroll; quill pen or stick to resemble pen

Costumes: All wear robes, sandals; women may wear head scarves

Music: Tape/Choir/Piano/Organ

Scriptures are taken from the *New International Version.*

Music plays two verses of "He Lives." Journalist enters rear stage left carrying scroll and pen during second verse and walks diagonally toward center stage very slowly. Journalist stops center stage, looking at scroll, and speaking when music ends.

JOURNALIST *(to audience):* Why? Why I ask you? Why? Why do they always do this to me—ask me to cover a story when the story is over? They did it when Jesus gave His Sermon on the Mount— sent me there ten days later! Whom did they think I was suppose to interview—a hill? And, when He fed the five thousand, was I there? Oh, sure I was—three weeks later! Not even a fish or a piece of bread to talk to—much less a person! Now this! Cover the resurrection, they tell me! Easy for them to say when Jesus' trial, crucifixion and resurrection happened over two months ago! Just what do those people at the *Jordan Journal* expect? Miracles, I guess!

(Peter enters stage right, with head bent, walks slowly toward Journalist; Journalist continues speaking.)

JOURNALIST: They should try it themselves sometime! Huh!

(Peter bumps into Journalist.)

PETER: Oh, I'm sorry! I wasn't looking where I was going!

JOURNALIST: As much my fault as yours! I wasn't paying any attention either!

PETER: My name is Peter—and you?

JOURNALIST: I'm a news person from the *Jordan Journal*.

PETER: You look downhearted and discouraged. What's the problem?

JOURNALIST: They sent me here to cover Jesus' resurrection! Can you believe it—two months after it happened! Ha!

PETER: Ah!

JOURNALIST: Say, you don't happen to know anything about it, do you?

PETER: As a matter of fact, I do! I was one of Jesus' disciples!

JOURNALIST: Oh, really! Would you mind telling me what you know?

PETER: Not at all!

JOURNALIST *(unrolling scroll and getting pen ready):* Wait a minute! I want to take this down! *(Pauses.)* Okay! Go on!

PETER: I was a fisherman when Jesus found me. He told me to follow Him and that He would make me a fisher of men. My name was Simon, but He called me Peter—that means "rock." He said to me, "I tell you that you are Peter, and on this rock I will build my church, and the gates of Hades will not overcome it" (Matthew 16:18).

JOURNALIST: Wow!

PETER: Yes! So I followed Jesus and was by His side until His trial. *(Sadly.)* That's when I betrayed Him.

JOURNALIST: How?

PETER: They asked me if I knew Him. Three times they asked and three times I denied it! Foolish me! I was afraid they would put me in prison or crucify me, too! I deeply regretted what I had done! I was sad—as you are now—only more so!

JOURNALIST: No wonder!

PETER: Yes! But I am comforted now because I know that Jesus rose from the dead and that He lives. I have dedicated my life to Him to do good works in His name for as long as I live!

JOURNALIST: Very interesting! You know, you should write a book about it some day!

PETER: Maybe I will!

JOURNALIST: Thanks for talking to me. You helped a lot with my story!

PETER: And it's helped me, too—talking about it. Good-bye, and take care!

(Peter exits slowly rear stage left; Journalist looks after Peter, then turns and speaks to audience.)

JOURNALIST: Well—that's a beginning! At least I'll have something to report!

(Journalist studies scroll; Secretary to Pilate enters stage right and follows path to Journalist; Secretary speaks on reaching Journalist.)

SECRETARY: Pardon me!

JOURNALIST *(looking up from scroll):* Oh! Excuse me! Am I in your way?

SECRETARY: Not really! You seemed to be concentrating so hard I was just wondering what you were doing!

JOURNALIST: Oh! Writing! I'm writing! I'm from the *Jordan Journal*, covering the resurrection of Jesus.

SECRETARY: But that happened months ago! It was the talk of the town, I can tell you!

JOURNALIST: Oh! You know something about the event?

SECRETARY: I most certainly do! I was right there in the thick of things!

JOURNALIST: And you are?

SECRETARY: Talia, secretary to Pilate, governor of Judea!

JOURNALIST: I see! Do you mind telling me about it? Do you mind if I write it down?

SECRETARY: Not at all! Not at all!

(Journalist gets ready to "write" on scroll.)

JOURNALIST: Go ahead!

SECRETARY: Well, you know that Pilate, as the Roman official in charge here, has to approve all death sentences. Most of the priests and Pharisees wanted Jesus put to death. I think they were jealous of Him, but don't quote me on that. *(Journalist nods.)* Anyway, three times they came to Pilate and three times he found Jesus not guilty—of anything. There was no doubt in Pilate's mind that Jesus was an innocent man. But the priests kept insisting. They even threatened Pilate by telling him they'd send word back to Rome saying what a weak, powerless governor he was.

THE TRUTH OF THE MATTER

JOURNALIST: So what did Pilate do?

SECRETARY: He gave in to them! I remember his words exactly. "'What is truth?' Pilate asked. With this he went out again to the Jews and said, 'I find no basis for a charge against him. But it is your custom for me to release to you one prisoner at the time of the Passover. Do you want me to release the king of the Jews'?" (John 18:38, 39). The crowd shouted "No, not him! Give us Barabbas!" Pilate turned Jesus over to them to be crucified.

JOURNALIST: Oh my!

SECRETARY: After Jesus was buried in a tomb and it was sealed with a huge boulder, Pilate placed guards there because there was fear the body would be removed by Jesus' followers. Three days after the crucifixion, the tomb was found open and empty!

JOURNALIST: But there were guards there!

SECRETARY: It seems they'd fallen asleep—asleep on the job, you could say. Their ranks were taken away from them as punishment for letting such a thing happen!

JOURNALIST: I see! Anything else?

SECRETARY: No! That's about all I can tell you. The *Jordan Journal* should have sent you sooner. You would have been able to talk to many more people then!

JOURNALIST: Don't I know it! But thanks for your information. It'll add something to my story.

(Secretary waves and exits rear stage left; Journalist looks after Secretary, then turns and speaks to audience.)

JOURNALIST: Well, I got a little more information! Still not enough to fill my column though.

(Journalist studies scroll; Nicodemus enters stage right, walks to Journalist and speaks.)

NICODEMUS: Hello, there. May I help you?

JOURNALIST *(looking up startled):* Oh! Hello. No. I was just looking at my writing.

NICODEMUS: Writing? Oh, I thought you were lost!

JOURNALIST: No. Just a journalist from the *Jordan Journal* gathering information on Jesus and the resurrection.

NICODEMUS: Somewhat late for that, wouldn't you say?

JOURNALIST: Somewhat!

NICODEMUS: I'm Nicodemus, a member of the Sanhedrin and a Pharisee. I don't know much about the resurrection, but I know a lot about Jesus. He was a teacher come from God. Would you like to hear about Him?

JOURNALIST *(getting scroll and pen ready):* Of course. Go on.

NICODEMUS: Most of the priests hated Jesus. He was gaining followers, and they were jealous of Him. So was I, at first. But then I
started listening to His teachings and His messages and I saw the
many miracles He performed. I began to believe in Him.

JOURNALIST: What did you do?

NICODEMUS: I went to Jesus, secretly, at night. It was very dangerous
for me to be seen with Him in the daytime. He taught me so
much. I learned wonderful things about Him and His kingdom.
From then on, I was a changed person. Then they crucified Him.

JOURNALIST: You must have felt awful!

NICODEMUS: Oh, yes! Joseph of Arimathea, a rich man, asked for the
body and gave up his own tomb so that Jesus would have a
proper burial place. I went with Joseph as he did this.

JOURNALIST: Weren't you taking a risk by doing that?

NICODEMUS: Yes—and to this day I am shunned by the other Pharisees. But I had to do it! I loved the Lord! (Pauses.) I'm sorry, but
that's all I know.

JOURNALIST: Don't be sorry. You've given me lots to go on and I
thank you for it.

NICODEMUS: Good! Then I'll leave you now to your writing.

(Journalist waves; Nicodemus exits rear stage left; Journalist turns and
speaks to audience.)

JOURNALIST: Well! It's getting better! I've got some more information
for my story! Good! (Looking around.) I don't see anyone else coming. Guess I'll move on! Maybe I'll meet up with someone down
the road!

(Journalist exits stage right. Music plays three verses of "In the Garden." Journalist reenters stage right during third verse, walks path to
center stage, looks at scroll, speaks to audience when music ends.)

JOURNALIST: Looks like I have just about enough for half a column so
far. If this is all I get, my editor will have to come up with a
filler—maybe some fashion or entertainment news. The whole
thing's the Journal's fault anyway for sending me so late to cover
the story. Still—what I have is interesting and will make good reading.

(Journalist studies scroll; Aide to Caiaphas enters rear stage left and
follows path to Journalist where Aide stops and speaks.)

AIDE: Good-day, stranger.

JOURNALIST: And to you.

AIDE: I don't believe I know you. I'm Vanta, aide to Caiaphas. And you?

JOURNALIST: A journalist—from the Jordan Journal—covering the resurrection of Jesus. Pleased to meet you.

AIDE: You're a bit late for that, don't you think?

JOURNALIST: What can I say? This is when the *Journal* sent me! Fortunately, I've interviewed three people so far who knew something about the event—not much—but something!

AIDE: I may be able to help you. Would you like to hear what I know?

JOURNALIST *(getting scroll and pen ready):* Of course. Tell me.

AIDE: Caiaphas, as you may or may not know, has been leader of the Sadducees and a high priest for many years. The Sadducees are a very rich and influential class in Judea. When Jesus came among us, they feared they would lose their influence and they certainly weren't willing to accept His message.

JOURNALIST: What did they do about it?

AIDE: The priests called a meeting and talked about the threat Jesus posed to them and how they could get rid of Him. Some suggested exile—sending Him out of the country forever. Others suggested prison. Then, Caiaphas spoke up and said, "You know nothing at all! You do not realize that it is better for you that one man die for the people than that the whole nation perish" (John 11:49, 50).

JOURNALIST: Did the other priests agree?

AIDE: Most of them. And those that didn't kept silent!

JOURNALIST: What happened next?

AIDE: The priests started plotting to kill Jesus. Of course, they were helped greatly by that fellow, Judas Iscariot, who was paid in silver pieces to point out Jesus while He was talking with His followers. After the guards had taken Jesus away, Judas tried to give back the money and undo his deeds, but it was too late. The priests just laughed at him!

JOURNALIST: Not a very pretty story.

AIDE: You may not believe so, but the priests had to protect their positions, don't you think?

JOURNALIST: I don't know about that.

AIDE: Well, I have told you all I know. I hope I've given you some information you can use in your story.

JOURNALIST: That you have!

(Aide exits stage right; Journalist looks after Aide, then turns and speaks to audience.)

JOURNALIST: Treacherous people! I hope I don't get in trouble for using this in my story. But I have to tell it! It's sensational news and that's what the *Journal's* readers want—sensationalism!

(Journalist studies scroll; Mary Magdalene enters rear stage left, walks to Journalist and speaks.)

MARY: The well is only a short way down the road.

JOURNALIST: Pardon?

MARY: The well! If you're looking for the well and want a drink, it's just down the path.

JOURNALIST: Oh! No! No! I wasn't looking for it. What I'm really looking for are some people who can give me information on the resurrection of Jesus. You see, I'm a journalist from the *Jordan Journal*.

MARY: Ah! The resurrection. That was two months ago, but I'll never forget it.

JOURNALIST: You were there?

MARY: Oh, yes!

JOURNALIST: Would you tell me about it?

MARY: Of course! The word must get out to all people.

JOURNALIST *(getting scroll and pen ready):* Thank you! Now, do you mind telling me your name?

MARY: Mary of Magdala. I'm often called Mary Magdalene.

JOURNALIST: Go ahead, please, Mary.

MARY: I knew Jesus a long time. I was a follower of His ever since the time He drove demons from my mind.

JOURNALIST: Demons?

MARY: Yes. Thoughts that confused me and spirits that had over-taken me.

JOURNALIST: I see! Go on, please.

MARY: I was wealthy, but I gave it all up to follow Jesus. I knew He was the King the moment He performed His miracle on me.

JOURNALIST: And were you at the crucifixion?

MARY: Yes. Yes. Sad. So sad. Then, on the third day after His death, I went to the cave where He was buried to anoint His body and see that the burial cloths were carefully wrapped around Him. But His body was gone!

JOURNALIST: How did you feel?

MARY: I was shocked. I kept asking myself—who could have done such a thing? Who could have taken His body? I was crying when I left the cave and I heard a voice asking me why I was crying. My eyes were so filled with tears that I thought it was the gardener, so I said, "Sir, if you have carried him away, tell me where you have put him, and I will get him" (John 20:15). And then Jesus spoke my name, Mary! I looked again and saw that it was Him! It was my Lord, Jesus!

JOURNALIST: So—you actually saw Jesus after He rose!

MARY: Oh, yes! And I cry no more because I know He's alive!

JOURNALIST: Remarkable.

MARY: Indeed. *(Pauses.)* I hope I've helped.

JOURNALIST: You have. You have.

MARY: I'm heading toward the well now. Would you like me to carry some water back to you?

JOURNALIST: No! No! I'm not the least bit thirsty.

MARY: Good-bye then, and be sure to tell the story of the resurrection to everyone.

JOURNALIST: The *Jordan Journal* has a large circulation. The word will spread!

(Mary nods and exits stage right; Journalist watches, then turns and speaks to audience.)

JOURNALIST: I can't believe it. I actually spoke with someone who saw Jesus after He rose from the dead. What a scoop. *(Pauses.)* It would be nice if I had a corroborating witness though. Ah—well—I'll just have to go with what I've got.

(Journalist studies scroll; Thomas enters rear stage left, walks to center stage and speaks to Journalist.)

THOMAS: Good-day to you.

JOURNALIST *(looking up from scroll):* Good-day.

THOMAS: Name's Thomas. I was hoping I'd meet someone along the way, someone to stop and talk with for a while.

JOURNALIST: I'm from the *Jordan Journal*—a journalist, you know—covering the resurrection of Jesus.

THOMAS: The resurrection! How could I ever have doubted it?

JOURNALIST: Pardon?

THOMAS: Just thinking out loud. Shall we sit for a while? My feet are tired. I could tell you what I know about the resurrection, if you like.

JOURNALIST: Sounds good.

(Both sit on stage; Journalist gets scroll and pen ready.)

THOMAS: I was a follower of Jesus. Believed what He said; believed He was Lord. When they crucified Him, I told the other disciples we should die along side Him too! You know, before He was crucified, Jesus had told us He would rise from the dead and be with us before going to His Father in Heaven, but after they buried Him and found His tomb empty, do you think I believed He had risen?

JOURNALIST: Did you?

THOMAS: Oh, no, not me! All the other disciples believed it—said they even saw Him—but did I believe? No! I had to have proof—proof of the resurrection—proof that I could see, touch and feel.

JOURNALIST: Did you ever get that proof?

THOMAS: Did I ever!

JOURNALIST: Tell me.

THOMAS: The disciples were meeting one night, behind locked doors because we were afraid the priest and Romans would be looking for Jesus' followers and do the same thing to us as they had done to Him. Then, suddenly, there He was—Jesus I mean! I still could not believe it. You can't imagine what Jesus did and what He said to me.

JOURNALIST: What?

THOMAS: He showed me His wounds from the crucifixion and said, "Put your finger here; see my hands. Reach out your hand and put it into my side. Stop doubting and believe" (John 20:27).

JOURNALIST: And what did you do?

THOMAS: Just what He told me to and then I knew, really knew, it was my Lord and God.

JOURNALIST: Totally awesome.

THOMAS: More than awesome—miraculous, I would say! But that's the way of God.

JOURNALIST: Umm!

THOMAS (standing up): I must be going now. (Journalist stands.) I've probably taken up too much of your time already.

JOURNALIST: Not at all! I've learned a lot from you.

THOMAS: I'm glad we met and I'm glad I had a chance to rest these (Pointing to feet.) tired feet.

JOURNALIST: I'm glad, too.

(Thomas and Journalist wave as Thomas exits stage right; Journalist turns and speaks to audience.)

JOURNALIST: I've got it. Corroboration. I've got it. Both Thomas and Mary reported seeing Jesus after He rose from the dead! (Looking at scroll.) This is going to make a great story. (Looking up.) So—once again the Jordan Journal sent me late to cover a story. Well, this isn't like the other times. This will show them. I'm going to insist on front-page coverage. Yes. That's what this story deserves! Now (Pauses.) for a headline! Let's see! (Pauses, thinking.) How about "He Lives?" (Pauses.) No. Too short. (Pauses.) Maybe "The Lord Rises!" (Pause.) No. I think someone's already used that in an earlier story. (Pauses, thinking.) I've got it. I've got it. A great headline—eye-catching and accurate. I'll headline it "The Truth of the Matter!" That tells it all!

(Music plays "Christ the Lord Is Risen Today." Journalist exits stage right. All return for curtain call as music plays.)

Something Different For Mom

Lillian Robbins

Characters
Narrator
Maggie
Amanda
Curt
Tasha
Wanda
Doris
Travis
Henry
Miriam
John
Mothers of children–six
(Stage hands to make scene changes in second act)

Costumes: Children in regular clothes. Clothes and make up for children to look like mothers and dad.

Props: Books for students, two yard benches, table, lamp, five chairs, lounge chair, broom, dust cloth, manicure set, hair brush or comb and spray, two present boxes, birdhouse, sewing supplies, dress, appropriate table setting, blueberry muffins, crown, soft drink, flowers, apron, muffin pan, trash can, potato peelings, potato, egg, flour, bandage, cereal, bowl, scarf, dishcloth.

Act I: Early morning on school grounds
Act II: In students' homes

Act I

(Maggie, Doris, and Travis sit on benches in school yard before the bell rings.)
MAGGIE: It's just always hard for me to decide what to give mother for Mother's Day. What are you going to get your mom, Doris?

DORIS: I really haven't thought about it much. You know Mother's Day is not this Sunday.

MAGGIE: I know, but things just have a way of creeping up on me.

TRAVIS: I've been thinking a lot about my mom. She's really had a hard time most of this school year.

DORIS: Yeah, it was tough on her when they cut her program in school. I still say it makes no sense. Why would they do that? Everybody here could see it was working.

MAGGIE: I think if they had given it a little more time, the school board would have been able to find some way to finance that program.

TRAVIS: With all the talk about better education, and then they cut some of the best programs. I don't get it.

MAGGIE: You know, Travis, I kept thinking they would place her somewhere else.

TRAVIS: Well, yeah, but nothing opened up for her.

CURT (enters): What are you guys talking about?

DORIS: Mother's Day. What great ideas do you have, Curt?

CURT: Who, me? You know I always depend on my sister for such things.

DORIS: Okay then. What great ideas does Amanda have?

CURT: You can ask her. Here she comes now.

(Amanda enters.)

TRAVIS (standing): Hey, Amanda, I've been wanting to talk to you about this weekend.

MAGGIE: Just hold it, Travis. We were talking about Mother's Day. We want to hear about Amanda's great idea.

AMANDA: Hi, guys. (Sits.) Well, I am working on a plan.

DORIS: A plan? Is it that complicated?

AMANDA: Not really. But I want us to do something a little different this year.

MAGGIE: Like what?

AMANDA: Well, Curt and I are going to cook breakfast for Mom.

TRAVIS: Cook breakfast? Curt can't cook.

MAGGIE: I bet he can pour a box of cereal in a bowl. (Laughs.)

CURT: Just wait a minute now. You may be surprised what I can do, especially if Amanda supervises.

WANDA (enters): It's almost time for the bell. What are you all up to?

TRAVIS: Actually, cooking breakfast.

WANDA: What? What did you say?

AMANDA: He's just being smart. We were talking about Mother's Day, and I said I was planning for Curt and me to cook breakfast.

WANDA: That would be special. You mean like a full course meal?

AMANDA: I'm not sure about that, but anyway the things Mom likes most.

WANDA: That's a neat idea. I wonder what I can do for my mom.

DORIS: I guess I better decide on something, too. I was thinking of just buying a scarf or something like that.

MAGGIE: I was trying to think of something special. You know, not just the same old thing like opening a box with a blouse in it or sending flowers.

DORIS: I always thought that was what you did for Mother's Day.

MAGGIE: It's okay, I guess. Well, I don't know. I just want to surprise Mom with something really different.

(Henry and Tasha enter.)

HENRY: It's time for the bell. I thought sure we were late.

TASHA: Mom's alarm clock didn't go off. We are just lucky that we woke up at all.

HENRY: Anyway, what's the news?

TRAVIS: Just talking about Mother's Day. What are you guys going to do for your mom?

TASHA: I'm working on it already. Mom wants me to learn how to be a good wife some day. She thinks that means learning to cook and sew and all that stuff.

DORIS: But that was in the old days. Nobody does much of that stuff anymore.

TASHA: Yeah, maybe you're right. But anyway, I'm learning to sew, and I love it. It just gives me a great feeling when I can make things with my own two hands. Wait until Mom sees this dress I'm making for her Mother's Day present. *(Bell rings.)*

TRAVIS *(as kids leave stage)*: I just don't know what I'll do for Mom. But it's got to be special.

Act II

Narrator introduces each scene.

Scene 1

Wanda's house—table, lamp, chair, rug on stage—some visible trash or dirt is in that area. A little to the side, Mom sits in a chair with a book.

WANDA'S MOM: This is super. I can just sit back and read this book. I've been dying to get into it for three weeks now

WANDA: You deserve a little time off, Mom. You have too much work to do anyway, with a full time job and everything.

MOM: But I like my job, Wanda. I don't have any complaints with that.

WANDA: You just ought to have somebody to help with housework.

MOM: I manage all right.

WANDA: But you never have time for yourself. So, today is your day. I know this is your cleaning day, and Mother's Day is not until Sunday, but this is just your special Mother's Day present. I'm going to clean for you.

MOM: You know, Wanda, I suppose it is time for you to take a little responsibility. It seems like you are growing up all of a sudden.

WANDA (*walking over to Mom*): I just want you to know how much I love you, Mom. (*Gives her a hug.*) Now you just settle down with your book and enjoy yourself. (*Mom starts to read. Wanda dusts furniture.*)

MOM (*looks up from book*): How are you doing, Dear?

WANDA: Oh, just fine. This cleaning deal is not too bad.

MOM: By the way, Wanda. This is just one room in the whole house you know.

WANDA: I know, but let's not talk about that now. (*Sweeps, looks around, sweeps dirt under rug.*) See, Mom, everything is finished in here.

MOM: Thanks, Wanda. Maybe both of us can take a little break with a glass of lemonade. Let's go in the yard.

WANDA: Super. I'm ready. (*Exit together.*)

Scene 2

Maggie's house—her mom sits as Maggie gives manicure.

MAGGIE'S MOM: Maggie, you know it has been a long time since I had a manicure.

MAGGIE: That's why I'm doing it for you now. It makes you feel so much better when you really look nice.

MOM: I guess so. I just don't have time for all those things.

MAGGIE: You must look just right for the concert tonight. Travis and I decided we would get these concert tickets for Mother's Day presents for our two moms.

MOM: I've always loved concerts, but it's been ages since I've been to one.

MAGGIE (*puts manicure set aside*): Now, that's done. Just hold your hands out carefully and give that polish a minute to dry. I just want to do a little touch up to your hair. (*Works with hair and sprays.*)

MOM: This is the most relaxing time for me. I have spent years doing my own shampoo and set. It's so good just to sit back and let somebody else take over.

MAGGIE: Here, Mom, look in this mirror. *(Hands mirror.)* How do you like this hairstyle?

MOM: You know what? It looks pretty good.

MAGGIE *(takes mirror and stands back to look):* And you look pretty, too, Mom. *(Gives her a hug.)* Happy Mother's Day even though it is a little early. You're the best mom in the world.

MOM: With the greatest daughter.

MAGGIE: Now if you run upstairs and put your jewelry on, you'll be ready in time. And let me go and choose the right necklace for that dress we chose. I want this to be a special night for you. *(Exit.)*

Scene 3

Tasha and Henry's house—Mom sits sewing.

TASHA *(enters):* Mom, I have a surprise for you.

TASHA'S MOM: I didn't hear you come in. That was the shortest shopping spree I've ever known you to have. Didn't you find anything you like?

TASHA: I just couldn't really get into it, Mom. I kept thinking about you.

MOM *(stops sewing):* Tasha, what is it? What's wrong?

TASHA: Nothing is wrong, Mom. I just have something special for you for Mother's Day this year, and I couldn't wait any longer. So here I am, and *(Steps back out door—reenters with box.)* here it is. Happy Mother's Day, Mom. *(Hugs her.)*

MOM: How sweet! I like surprises. *(Opening box.)* You went shopping for me.

TASHA: Not shopping, Mom. *(Mom holds up dress.)* I made this dress for you.

MOM *(holds dress up to her):* You made this dress? Oh, how wonderful, Tasha. You made this dress. It's beautiful! Oh, it's just beautiful. And you really made it? *(Gives Tasha hug.)*

TASHA: That's the reason I've spent so much extra time at school. Mrs. Kent let me work on it there so I would be able to surprise you.

MOM: And surprise me, you did! *(Looks at seams.)* I'm so proud of you, Tasha. You're going to be a good seamstress.

TASHA: I don't know about that. But I will be able to make things when I want to.

HENRY *(enters):* What's all the fuss about in here?

MOM *(holds dress up):* Look, Henry, Tasha made me a dress for Mother's Day.

HENRY: I knew she was doing that. That's a pretty dress, Mom. It'll look beautiful on you. But, of course everything always does.

MOM: Oh, go on, Henry. You and your flattery.

HENRY: Just wait a minute. *(Goes out and returns with a birdhouse.)* I can use my hands, too, you know. I know how much you enjoy bird watching so I made this for you.

MOM *(puts dress aside—takes birdhouse):* Henry, a birdhouse. Oh, how wonderful. Now my little friends will have a place to get in out of the cool weather when they want to. They can nest in their own little house right here in my yard. *(Gives Henry a hug.)* Thanks, son. It is so cute.

HENRY: I had a hard time deciding about the color. I thought to myself, if you make a blue birdhouse for blue birds and a red house for red birds, then what color would you use for sparrows?

MOM: I don't think it really matters, Henry. This is just right.

HENRY: I thought maybe you'd like it.

MOM: Come on, you two, let's put it up in the backyard. *(Exit.)*

Scene 4

Curt and Amanda's house—Curt and Amanda are preparing breakfast.

AMANDA: Mom, Dad, everybody, come on to breakfast. *(Little sister Miriam runs in.)*

MIRIAM: May I come in now?

CURT: Sure, Miriam. It's all ready.

(Mom and Dad enter.)

MOM: I think this is just the best idea. I get to eat without doing a thing.

AMANDA: That's because it's your special day.

CURT: Just sit at the head of the table, Mom.

AMANDA: And you'll wear this crown, because you are queen for the day. *(Mom sits—Amanda places crown.)* Okay, everybody, have a seat. Dad, if you'll say the prayer, we'll be ready.

DAD: Thank You, Lord, for Your bountiful blessings, for the food to nourish our bodies, and most of all for these precious children and their wonderful mother. Amen.

MOM *(to Dad):* That's sweet, John.

AMANDA: Mom, I know your favorite is blueberry muffins, and we fixed those little cheese things you like, too. *(Mom serves plate— others follow.)*

Mom: It looks great. *(Takes a bite.)* And tastes delicious. Curt, I didn't know you could cook.

Curt: Well, I just did what Amanda told me to do. *(To Amanda.)* But just this time, Amanda. Don't get the idea you can start bossing me around.

Miriam: When is my turn, Amanda?

Amanda: Well, why not now?

Miriam: Mom, I have a special Mother's Day gift for you, too. I learned this song I want to sing for you. *(Sings an appropriate song.)*

Mom *(gets up from table, hugs Miriam):* Honey, that was so beautiful. I know you have a good voice, and it's even better when it's just for me.

Miriam: Happy Mother's Day, Mom. I love you. *(They sit and eat.)*

Dad: Well, dear, I don't want to put a shadow on their moment for you, so my present will just come a little later.

Mom: Thanks, everybody. It's kinda nice being queen for a day. I guess it's good that Mother's Day comes only once a year. I may get spoiled by all this attention.

Amanda: We just want you to know how much we love you, Mom.

Curt: Yeah, Mom, we really do.

Miriam: And me, too.

(As they get up from table, Mom gathers them in her arms.)

Mom: And I love all of you. Now if we hurry, we'll just be in time for church. *(Exit.)*

Scene 5

Travis' house. Travis enters with bag of food and flowers for table—whistles, hums or sings as he prepares—puts out Chinese food.

Travis' Mom *(from offstage):* Travis, did you call me?

Travis: Not yet, Mom. I'm not quite ready.

Mom *(moment later from offstage):* Travis, should I wear the blue or that pretty red dress?

Travis: I think the blue will be good for the concert.

Mom *(offstage):* Okay. I'm almost ready.

Travis: I think that's it. Food, flowers, and oh, yes, Mom likes a soft drink with Chinese food. *(Pours soft drink.)* Okay, Mom.

(Mom enters.)

Travis *(takes Mom's hand):* Welcome, my lady, to the famous Chinese restaurant of the Chandlers.

Mom: Pleased to be here, my man.

Travis: We have a special table for you. Right this way, please.

(Holds chair for Mom.) We are serving some of our most famous recipes this evening, just for you.

MOM: I'm honored. This is going to be a lovely evening.

TRAVIS: And *(Points to centerpiece.)* fresh flowers just as you like them.

MOM: They're beautiful! *(Dabs at eyes.)* I think I'm going to cry.

TRAVIS: But this is a happy occasion, celebrating the best mom in the world with dinner and a concert with a dear friend. We don't need tears, we need laughter.

MOM *(laughs)*: Oh, Travis, you are such a dear. I love you.

TRAVIS: And I love you, Mom. You're the greatest. I'll say the prayer, Mom. Thank You, Lord, for my mom and for all the wonderful blessings we enjoy. Thank You for this food to nourish our bodies. Amen.

MOM *(eats)*: Ummm, this is really delicious. I didn't know you could cook such good Chinese food.

TRAVIS: You didn't know you had a special chef in the house? Well, this is just a special menu for a special lady.

MOM: And a special son. *(They eat.)*

TRAVIS *(looks at watch)*: Mom, I don't want to rush you, but it's almost time for Maggie's mom to come by.

MOM *(stands)*: Thanks, Travis. It was a delicious dinner. And I'm sure we'll have a lovely time at the concert.

TRAVIS: Happy Mother's Day, Mom. I love you.

MOM: And I love you. You've made me a very happy mother. *(Hugs him.)* Come and help me choose the best earrings for tonight. *(Exit.)*

Scene 6

Doris' house—items to prepare breakfast are on the table.

DORIS *(wearing an apron)*: Let's see, now, what do I do first? I want to make blueberry muffins, eggs benedict, and hash browns. Mom always said she would have somebody serve her breakfast in bed if she was rich. So today, for a special Mother's Day present, I'm going to serve her breakfast in bed. *(Some potatoes already peeled, peels are piled on plastic bag. Doris peels last potato—pretends to cut finger.)*

DORIS: Mom, where is that spray you use for cuts and scratches?

MOM *(from offstage)*: Look in that cabinet near the pantry.

DORIS *(steps offstage—comes back putting on bandage)*: Mom, where do I put these potato peelings?

Mom *(offstage):* In the trash can, but you can wait until everything is finished and put all the scraps in there at one time.

Doris: Maybe I should get these muffins mixed before I cook the hash browns. It'll take muffins longer to cook. *(Looks at recipe—puts flour in bowl, but spills it all on floor.)* Oh, dear, what a mess. I don't have time to get this up now. *(Sweeps flour aside.)* Mom, where are the muffin pans?

Mom: On the top shelf behind the door.

Doris *(steps offstage, back with muffin pans):* Let me see. I have to add one egg to the flour. Mom, do you use the whole egg for blueberry muffins or just the whites?

Mom *(offstage):* Whole egg.

Doris: What about the cholesterol?

Mom *(offstage):* We don't get much cholesterol in anything else.

Doris: Okay. Thanks. *(Breaks egg, and drops on top of peels.)* Oh, no! What a mess. This cooking deal is not so great. And I don't have another egg. What can I do? *(Looks around.)* I know. *(Gets trash can from corner, pulls everything off table into can, wipes table, puts cereal in bowl.)*

Doris: Mom, could you come down here?

Mom: Sure, be right there.

Doris: I'm just no good at this cooking, Mom. *(Gives her a hug.)* But I love you anyway.

Mom: It's okay, Honey. You know I eat cereal every morning.

Doris: But I really wanted this Mother's Day to be special.

Mom: It is special, because I have you for a daughter.

Doris: Mom, you're the greatest. Just have a seat for your favorite breakfast meal.

Mom: Delighted. *(Sits.)* This is just what I wanted.

Doris: But wait a minute. *(Exits, returns with present.)* There is something I'm good at—shopping. *(Hands present.)* Happy Mother's Day, Mom.

Mom: Thanks, Sweety. *(Opens box, holds up scarf.)* Oh, it's beautiful. You are such a good shopper, Doris. I just love this scarf. *(Hugs her.)*

Narrator *(as other cast members return to stage):* And so it is with families all across the nation. Mother's Day is celebrated in many ways. But the important thing is to show your mother how special she is, and how much you love her. That show of affection will make her day great.

Cast: Happy Mother's Day everybody!

I Can't Believe My Father

Iris Gray Dowling

Monologue based on Luke 15:11-32.

Speaker is the Elder Son, brother of the Prodigal Son

(Speaking to self; uses hand gestures of disgust.)

I know I was harsh with my father, but I get so angry when I see him pull back the curtains and gaze out the windows every day. Then he turns away disappointed and doesn't eat any breakfast. I told him he's wasting his time. Jarib won't come back after what he's done.

I said to him, "Father, if you saw the places he's been, the things he's done, and the cruddy people he's spent the night with, you wouldn't want him back." Other times I added, "Why did you give him all his money to squander? You know he always had a free spirit. Think how I could have used the money to make a profit for us. But, no, you had to give it to him. Don't you know he's having a good time drinking and entertaining his immoral friends? We've got a business to run. We need to get on with our lives."

I tried to help him see the truth. *(Pauses; repeats to himself.)* Father, you think he'll come home when he's out of money? And you'll accept him back? Don't you think you've given him enough to squander? *(Pauses.)* You think he really cares about you? *(Pauses.)* I'll never understand your way of thinking. You know what he needs, don't you? He needs to learn to work, like I do. *(Pauses.)*

I saw Father wasn't listening to anything I said. He can't think of anyone but Jarib. He doesn't appreciate me and all the work I do for him. *(Points to self.)*

Of course, Father assures me I'm important to him. He says he loves me. His words were, "I'll always have you. I can trust you to stay here and take care of the farm." It's nice to know he trusts me.

Why would Jarib want to come back here. I hope he's too proud for that. *(Sarcastically.)* He got all he's entitled to.

(Pauses; hands over eyes to look in distance.) Oh, no! I see someone in the distance. Who could be coming so early in the day? *(Pauses; puts hand above eyes.)* He walks like Jarib. That scoundrel! He's coming back to get my inheritance too! *(Pauses; acts fidgety.)*

I wonder if Father's looking out the window. Should I go in and tell him? *(Pauses; shakes head.)* No, I'll wait. *(Pauses.)* Maybe I can tell Jarib to go back where he came from so Father will never know. *(Pauses.)* Look! *(Hand above eyes.)* He's coming closer. *(Pauses; acts fidgety.)* I guess I'd better see what Father is doing. *(Pretends to enter door and is startled as he meets Father.)*

Oh! *(Pauses; startled.)* Father! I didn't expect you to be so close to the door. Were you looking for me? *(Points to self; pause.)* No? *(Pauses.)* You saw a person coming down the road? *(Pauses.)* You saw him from the minute he appeared in the distance? *(Pauses.)* Oh! You think it is Jarib? *(Pauses.)* You want me to tell the servants to kill our best calf and prepare a big dinner? After what he did, you're going to welcome him like that? He doesn't deserve to be rewarded. *(Pauses; turns head away from him; speaks in disgust.)* When will I ever get a feast for staying here faithfully working day after day? *(Pauses.)* What did I say? Oh, nothing, Father. *(Pauses.)*

Father, don't you know he could bring diseases to us? You realize he's been living in unsanitary places? *(Pauses.)* Just do what you say as quickly as possible? *(Pauses.)* You didn't hear a word I said, did you? *(Pauses; moves to SR.)*

(Shakes head.) Humm! I'll never understand my father. Why doesn't he think? I suppose he'll let that dirty, ragged, double-crossing beggar come back in this house. He'll give him back his own room to live like he always did. He'll eat all the best food like nothing ever happened. It's not fair!

(Stomps foot.) Well, I'm not going to this party. I don't want to see any friend of prostitutes. I'll have no part of merrymaking over him. *(Pauses; thinks.)*

What am I going to say when Father comes out to see where I am? First, I'll say I had to check on the animals in the barn. Then I'll just tell him, "Father, I worked many years without a vacation. I never refused anything you wanted me to do. You never praised me for doing a good job. You never had a party for me and my friends. I should have rebelled and had fun, too. I should have spent your money and then you would give me a party too." *(Pauses; listens.)*

(Show a break in time by turning to face backstage; then slowly turn to face front again.)

My father came out and talked kindly to me. I didn't have the heart to say those things I'd planned. He must have known how I felt. He said all he has belongs to me, that I had nothing to be upset about.

He put his arm around me and walked me into the party. Then my brother hugged and kissed me, and asked my forgiveness.

Now I know why my father forgave Jarib. Jarib didn't act rebellious or haughty as I thought he would. He acted more like one of the servants. At last, I understand why my father did all those things for him. I understand his words, "Jarib was dead and is alive again; he was lost and is found." *(Pauses.)*

What a heavenly father we have—one who forgives like that!